D1011537

Stirring It Up

Stirring It Up

HOW TO MAKE MONEY AND
SAVE THE WORLD

Gary Hirshberg

New York

Library of Congress Cataloging-in-Publication Data is available upon request.

ISBN: 978-1-4013-0344-0

Hyperion books are available for special promotions, premiums, or corporate training. For details contact Michael Rentas, Proprietary Markets, Hyperion, 77 West 66th Street, 12th floor, New York, New York 10023, or call 212-456-0133.

FIRST EDITION

10 9 8 7 6 5 4 3 2 1

For Meg, whose partnership and love
make the impossible possible, and for
Alex, Ethan, and Danielle,
who give me hope and purpose.

Contents

A Note on the Production of This Book

Through a partnership with NativeEnergy, a privately held energy company (www.nativeenergy.com), the estimated global warming gas emissions resulting from the production of this book are being offset by an investment in a manure digester at the Warner Family Dairy Farm in Narvon, Pennsylvania. Over its operating life, the digester will capture and use the methane—a powerful global warming gas—given off by the manure the farm's cows produce to instead produce electricity and heat energy. For more information on how the emissions were calculated, the offset project, or how you can offset your emissions, visit www.stonyfield.com/stirringitup.

Hyperion saved the following resources by printing *Stirring It Up* on New Leaf Pioneer 100 for the text and Neenah Environment 100 for the jacket. Both papers are made with 100% post-consumer waste fiber versus virgin fiber.

TREES:
67 fully grown

WATER
28,769 gallons

ENERGY:
49 million Btu

SOLID WASTE:
3,209 pounds

GREENHOUSE GASES:
6,322 pounds

Foreword

While sweating through my workout at a local gym recently, something caught my eye. There, outside in the parking lot, stood a varied collection of compact cars. It struck me that just a year ago, I'd glanced out the same window at rows crammed with big SUVs. Ours is a middle-income New Hampshire community, and I had wondered then how the owners of those rolling Parthenons of Excess were coping with rising fuel costs. Now, on this particular morning, I saw only one lonely SUV sticking out like a white elephant among the herd of VW Jettas, Toyota Corollas, and at least five or six hybrid Priuses.

What had brought about this heartening turn to green? I wondered. Had all of my neighbors been won over after hearing Al Gore lay out the frightening facts of climate change in his film *An Inconvenient Truth*? Had our local churches persuaded their parishioners that saving the planet was covered under the divine directives written on Moses's stone tablets? Or, perhaps, had a wave of guilt, morality, or newfound virtue washed over my fellow townsfolk?

In truth, the explanation is far less dramatic—and one you may already have guessed since it is affecting every city, town, and village in America. This seemingly sudden turnabout has less to do with a moral awakening than with a spike in gasoline prices.

My hunch about the prime reason my neighbors had changed their car preferences was borne out in a June 2007 poll by the Associated Press, in which 46 percent of Americans said soaring gasoline prices would cause them "serious hardship"; 66 percent said they planned to reduce their driving; and 47 percent said they were planning to buy a new fuel-efficient car.

These numbers represent the kind of ecologically pleasing conversion the Sierra Club could only dream of in times past. And it's all because the flow of greenbacks out of consumers' pockets has brought the notion of going "green" back into vogue. The speed and effectiveness of this little revolution have been both breathtaking and absolute.

As George Bernard Shaw once said, "Virtue is insufficient temptation." Our planet will not be saved by preaching principles and exerting moral suasion. After more than three decades spent working in the environmental movement, I am convinced that economic self-interest—whether it is achieved by saving, earning, or both—is the most powerful, if not the *only,* force capable of bringing about the future we need in time to make a difference to the well-being of Mother Earth.

And here's the good news: Ecologically sound practices are also economically sound over the long term. Indeed, as the examples in this book will show, saving the planet can prove profitable in both a fiscally narrow sense and in a much broader context of job creation and greatly expanded economic development. Addressing climate and environmental challenges will give twenty-first-century businesspeople and ordinary citizens the chance to grasp what Pogo called "insurmountable opportunities," possibilities that may exceed anything humankind has ever seen before.

This book is an unabashedly optimistic and hopeful embrace of those opportunities. And lest you dismiss my enthusiasm as nothing more than the delusional rants of a child of the sixties, I hasten to remind you that I am a passionate capitalist who has created thousands of jobs and millions of dollars of capital appreciation for hundreds of investors in Stonyfield Farm. I measure progress with hard numbers and productive assets listed on balance sheets. I have little patience for big talk and no do.

Nor is my perspective an outgrowth of my political leanings. Rather, it is a practical economic stance honed by several decades of trial and error in my hard-fought journey from windmill builder and antinuclear protester to CE-Yo of a profitable company. And, importantly, my view has been refined by the inspirational accomplishments of more than a dozen remarkable businesspeople whose stories are captured in these pages.

As this century begins, we find our nation and our species mired in polarizing debates defined as red versus blue, rich versus poor, the developed world versus the still-developing one, local versus global. And each passing day of gridlock takes us closer to the precipice of environmental catastrophe even as our modern-day prophets, the scientific community, warn of the consequences. Without decisive and immediate action, they say, our children—indeed, all life on this planet—will be deprived of the clean air and water and the health-giving food that prior generations have taken for granted. The Intergovernmental Panel on Climate Change made clear in early 2007 the urgency when it said that we have but one decade in which to establish the new trajectory of carbon emissions needed to forestall a mid-century calamity.

With such ominous warnings from a respected body of scientists, why the polarity and gridlock? When it comes to the planet, too many participants in the debate subscribe to the myth that ecology and economy are somehow mutually exclusive, or that big is bad and small is inherently good. And advocates for each position are seemingly more focused on proving themselves right and their opponents wrong than on actually averting the looming crisis.

Such behavior is both pathetic and shameful—and it's also intellectually dishonest. Globalization itself is not inherently bad; what is bad is our long tradition of allowing the rich to exploit the poor. Stories abound of ecologically and economically successful endeavors that promote sustainability and enable all parties—from suppliers to farmers to investors and consumers—to prosper. And in these success stories, the biggest winner of all is the planet.

There can be no doubt or argument that one of the great contributors to environmental degradation is our excessive consumption, particularly in the United States. Experts have estimated that if everyone on the planet consumed energy, water, and natural resources at the rates Americans do, we'd need three Earths to sustain us. Clearly, any rational steps to shrink our environmental and climate footprints must begin with reductions in consumption. There are many texts, guides, and resources that exist to help us all reduce our gluttonous ways. As the adage goes, we need to *reduce* first, then *reuse* what we've had to consume, and then *recycle* what we have consumed but cannot reuse.

If I were writing a book on how to reduce our environmental

footprint, my first three chapters would focus on why and how we must reduce our consumptive habits. I would also have a chapter arguing that the government must levy taxes on consumption rather than income, because I believe that would be the fairest and most effective incentive for change on a broad scale.

But I'll save those points for another book; this one has a different focus. The reality is that even after we have cut our consumption, we will still consume. And that is my topic here. How we consume makes all the difference. Conscientious consumption of goods that have lower environmental footprints sends a powerful message to the businesses that produce them (and the ones that don't). By rewarding those companies' efforts to reduce their resource use, we can wield enormous power. American businesses spend many hundreds of millions of dollars on market research to learn about our consumption choices; these findings are the nectar that fuels them. And as the messages come back that large numbers of us want less waste, fewer toxins, and more renewable resources used in the production of goods, the changes will follow.

Every one of us must unquestionably reduce our resource consumption and the size of our environmental footprints. None of us can afford to avoid scrutinizing and changing our lifestyles. But the scientists tell us that, especially with regard to climate change, we have a lot less time than we had previously thought to start solving the problem. And after three decades straddling the worlds of business and environmental activism, I have concluded that the quickest and most powerful way to effect large-scale change is to use our purchasing power as both carrot and stick to prod business to get to work saving the planet.

It's time we jettisoned the notion that global and local are conflicting positions. We need to and can think and act "glocally" by combining our best can-do, entrepreneurial spirit with a practical awareness that our traditional linear approach simply does not work in an inherently cyclical natural world. Certainly, a linear approach does not produce any true gains, as business leaders themselves have come to recognize. Rather, it produces something unknown in nature, and that is enormously costly waste. So, like practitioners of *aikido* who learn not to block opposing forces but rather to join the incoming thrusts and redirect them toward a different outcome, we need to act harmoniously with our planet by engaging the forces of capitalism to help create truly sustainable societies.

I will be the first to admit that the unceasing alarms about impending ecological catastrophe send most people heading straight to the nearest bar or to some other diversionary setting where they can drown out the depressing pronouncements of the doomsayers. I also know that even the most committed of us feel a certain degree of impotence when we consider the scale of the problems and the forces at play. Sure, there are numerous things each of us could and should do every day that would make a difference to our planet. But who among us has the energy and dedication to do every single thing we can, especially when the deleterious effects of egregious pollution by giant industrial and commercial operations are visible for all to see? It's more than a little discouraging to be cruising along the highway in my Prius and watch a Hummer blow by, let alone a monstrous diesel-powered tractor-trailer that leaves a cloud of soot in its wake. Our politicians and industrial titans get the same feeling when they see the economies of India and China exploding in a fossil-fuel-powered burst of energy. Why should we voluntarily make expensive investments to lessen our industrial production of carbon gases, they think, when China builds a new carbon-spewing coal plant every week?

And even though all the talk about greening is music to my ears, I will readily concede that the guilt-tripping admonitions about changing lightbulbs and lowering thermostats feel like a less-than-effective salve for what ails us. Hearing these sirens reminds me of a line uttered by my favorite philosopher, Lily Tomlin, who says, "No matter how cynical I get, it's hard to keep up."

But don't get me wrong. While I am deeply sympathetic to the psychological hurdles such incremental steps toward sustainability present, I am also a deep believer in the power of each of us to make a difference. The anthropologist Margaret Mead was right when she said, "Never doubt that a small group of thoughtful, committed citizens can change the world. Indeed, it is the only thing that ever has." But thirty-plus years after committing myself to being useful to the planet and twenty-four years after starting in business, I've come to a few hardheaded conclusions:

- It's going to take a lot more than moral rectitude and virtuous principles to set us on a truly sustainable path.
- Business is the most powerful force on the planet; it got us into this mess and is the only force strong enough to get us out.
- Most environmental problems exist because business has not made solving them its priority.

- Only when the solutions to our environmental problems are accompanied by profitable, commercial strategies for enacting them will the business world get on board.

In short, planetary fixes will never get off the ground unless they are part of a profit-making venture. But here's the really cool thing: Sustainable ideas can and do work.

And here's another cool thing: All it takes to make use of ecologically sound and profitable ideas is willpower.

And here's the coolest thing of all: Many, many people are doing just that, right now—including those of us who labor under the Stonyfield banner.

Indeed, my hopes and inspiration are reinforced by the hundreds of hardworking colleagues who have helped to create Stonyfield Farm. I am especially grateful to my co-creators, Samuel and Louise Kaymen, and to the many current and former members of my Executive Team, particularly the two longtimers, Steve Inamorati and Kasi Reddy. You are all magicians and alchemists, and I honor you. Special gratitude goes to my sister, Nancy Hirshberg, our vice president of natural resources; my chief of staff, Mary Townsend; and my chief operating officer, Diane Carhart, all of whom have not only motivated me but also given me the freedom to organize my three decades of insights and knowledge into a form that has allowed this book to become a reality.

I also wish to thank my colleagues at Groupe Danone, especially Daniel Carasso, Franck Riboud, Bernard Hours, Emmanuel Faber, Anne Thevenet-Abitbol, Dirk Van de Put, Jordi Constans, and Juan-Carlos Dalto, as well as the many others there who have become believers in the organic way of life and business. They have boosted my confidence that the largest corporations can become powers for good.

There are so many other dear friends, peers, and fellow travelers who have challenged and inspired me to see that we are limited only by our imaginations. Yvon and Malinda Chouinard of Patagonia; Gun Denhart of Hanna Andersson; George Siemon and Theresa Marquez of Organic Valley; Ben Cohen of Ben & Jerry's; Jeff Swartz of Timberland; Walter Robb, Betsy Foster, and John Mackey of Whole Foods; Mike Funk of United Natural Foods; Steve McDonnell of Applegate Farms; Andrew Shapiro of GreenOrder; Steve Pimentel of Costco; and Linda Mason, Roger Brown, Peter Roy, Steve Demos, Lex Alexander, Seth Goldman, Paul Hawken, Nell Newman, Jeffrey Hollender, Joel Makower, Lisa Witter, Bob Burke, Drake Sadler, Eric Schlosser, and others too numerous to mention. I've profiled many of you in these pages, but mere words could never adequately express my admiration and gratitude for your contributions.

I must also acknowledge Steve Palmer, Stonyfield's attorney for a zillion years, who kept me from getting into too much mischief or, for that matter, jail. And this book would still be swirling around in my head were it not for my wonderful agent, Helen Rees, who kicked my butt into gear, and my cowriters at Wordworks Inc., Donna Carpenter and Maurice Coyle, and their capable colleagues Ruth Hlavicek, Larry Martz, Cindy Butler Sammons, and Robert Shnayerson, who dragged me kicking and screaming to my computer keyboard to actually finish the manuscript. I am also indebted to the talented people at Hyperion, Leslie Wells, Bob Miller, Ellen Archer, Will Schwalbe, and the rest of the team.

Behind every success is usually an amazing mom, and, in

my case, there are two—Louise Hirshberg, who pretty much single-handedly raised five children and launched several business careers, thus proving beyond a doubt that absolutely anything is possible, and my mom-in-law, Doris, who never gave up on me. Without the two of you, my work would not have been possible. And my father, Howard, who taught me much that is good and bad about business.

And, finally, it is my amazing and beautiful wife, Meg, and our radiant children, Alex, Ethan, and Danielle (my *petite Napoleone*) who give meaning and purpose to my every day. Your love and support mean everything to me.

Stirring It Up

1

Natural Profits

For more than twenty-five years, I've been turning green ideas into greenbacks, and if that seems far-fetched, I'm here to tell you that nature and business are born allies—potentially the richest partnership in the history of capitalism.

Sustainability is the key to that alliance. A sustainable system is nature's version of the proverb "waste not, want not." Our solar-powered planet doesn't exude waste. Our planet is a wondrous system of interdependent processes that nourish themselves. In my view, the more any business emulates this model, the more it can generate true wealth for its owners, customers, and all humans.

How I became an eco-entrepreneur is a story that began in the late 1970s when I was executive director of the New Alchemy Institute, an ecological research and education center on Cape Cod, Massachusetts. We built a solar-heated greenhouse that used no fossil fuels, herbicides, pesticides, or chemical fertilizers. Yet it produced enough food to feed ten people three meals per day, 365 days per year. Even when the yard was covered with snow, it was toasty inside—a haven for everything from birds and bees to bananas, figs, and papayas. Tanks of water absorbed sunlight by day and radiated heat at night. Each tank raised about one hundred pounds of fish per year. Their waste fertilized plants, which, in turn, provided food for the herbivorous fish. Wind systems provided electrical and mechanical power.

All this seemed to be a worthy achievement to this young idealist until 1982, when I visited my mother, then a senior buyer at Disney's Epcot Center in Orlando, Florida. There I rammed into one of those epiphanies that change your life forever.

We toured the Land Pavilion where sponsor Kraft Foods was touting its vision of future farming. In tribute to the blessings of supposedly endlessly fertile land and unlimited resources, Kraft displayed, in a building both heated and cooled by fossil fuels, rivers of chemical fertilizers, herbicides, and pesticides swooshing around the naked roots of anemic-looking plants grown hydroponically in plastic tubes. In this paean to fertility, there was not a single grain of actual soil. Natural farming is all about creating great dirt, rich with nutrients. This was a cartoon scene of chemistry gone mad. As I saw it, nothing grown the Kraft way would sustainably nourish a laboratory rat, much less soil itself.

Kraft underscored its bizarre message with "Kitchen Kabaret," a pseudo-musical featuring the four food groups and Bonnie Appetit, the show's only live character. The other "actors" were animatronic robots named Miss Cheese, Miss Ice Cream, Miss Yogurt, and the like, who sang lyrics I wish I could forget:

Your taste buds I'll appease.
I know how to please.
It's known that I am too good for words.
Oh, isn't that right, big boy?

As bad as the lyrics were, I left feeling that the singing foodstuffs were secretly humming a very different and troubling tune:

Just buy Velveeta, please.
So what if it's not real cheese?
Real is what we'll say it is,
And Mother Nature's on her knees.

Every day, twenty-five thousand people paid to see this spectacle—more than visited my own New Alchemy Institute in a year. After viewing the Kraft-sponsored pavilion twice myself, I came away deeply disturbed.

While stewing about all this, I had a eureka flash that eventually shaped my life, built my company, and led me to write this book. I blurted out to my mother: "I have to become Kraft."

Don't misunderstand. I was still convinced that Kraft was crazy and only sustainable practices could save the planet. But now I faced the reality that people like me were unheard voices preaching to ourselves in an uncaring world. To change anything, we needed the leverage of powerful businesses like Kraft. If we had their cash and clout, people would listen and begin to make changes, which led to my key point: To persuade business to adopt sustainable practices, I would have to prove they were profitable.

Ever since, the challenge of proving that sustainability pays—and hugely—has driven my career. Somewhat to my own surprise, I have succeeded. After years of work and many experiments, I have discovered that sustainable practices not only make money, but are invariably more profitable than conventional business methods. Now I want to share what I've learned and persuade other businesspeople to join the cause.

Once corporations like Kraft realize that businesses can derive big profits from cleaning up the planet and operating in green, sustainable ways, the battle will be won. Business is the most powerful force on Earth. Unlike governments, which are usually bound by politics and convention, business can lead. Unlike churches, community groups, and nonprofits, business has money to back up its ideas. It can act quickly, get rules changed, and overcome entrenched interests. In one of those ironic twists that make life so interesting, the same boundless thirst for profit that got the planet into trouble can also get us out of it.

Efficiency Isn't

The first step is to understand that many widely held assumptions are wrong. Take the notion that modern agribusiness is a model of efficiency. Some analysts calculate that typical food producers use ten to fifteen calories of fossil-fuel energy to produce every single calorie of food energy they sell. By any standard, economic or environmental, that's ridiculous—a suicidal ride to bankruptcy via inefficiency. But because the industry's conventional accounting method adds up only dollars, not energy—or, for that matter, any so-called externalized costs, such as resource depletion, pollution, or the demise of farmers—agribusiness is wrongly deemed "efficient."

This story line, nicely told in Michael Pollan's excellent book *The Omnivore's Dilemma*, began with the advent of synthetic fertilizer, first developed in the United States using ammonium nitrate left over from the production of explosives in World War II. Synthetic fertilizer combines vast quantities of nitrogen with a fossil fuel, usually natural gas. It makes it possible to grow genetically identical plants on hundreds of thousands of acres, year after year, apparently without concern for wearing out the soil.

That's the seemingly good news. Absent the need to rotate crops or leave a field fallow to replenish depleted nutrients, farmers are free to practice monoculture. Genetically modified hybrid corn, a voracious consumer of nitrogen, is now produced on a huge scale. The corn farm operates like a factory, transforming vast quantities of fossil-fuel energy into food energy.

There's a catch: The fertility that comes in bags and tankers depends on petroleum energy stored up aeons ago from the remains of dead plants and animals. It is nonrenewable, in contrast to the ongoing natural process that breeds soil-borne microorganisms, which feed on the roots of a rotating crop of legumes such as soybeans and make nutrition available to plants. In other words, monoculture is not sustainable. It's the opposite of nature's self-supporting systems. It's a stranger to the soil it uses. Instead of enriching the land, monoculture just rents it for a season and then checks out, like motel guests in the morning, leaving the room a mess for the maid to clean up.

Fossil fuels are needed to make the synthetic fertilizer, of course, and more fuel is spent to power the equipment that plants, harvests, and carries the corn and other crops to market. But something else happens when agribusiness upsets the balance of nature with scientific meddling. It turns out that feeding plants with synthetic nitrogen, which leaves them deficient in certain micronutrients, in turn makes them more vulnerable to pests. The factory farmer caught up in this counterintuitive approach reacts by dousing his crop and the soil beneath it with chemical herbicides and pesticides, wasting still more fossil fuel in the process.

Intuitively, a farmer might be expected to protect his sources of fresh, clean water and conserve topsoil. But with no need to plant cover crops to restore nitrogen and nutrients, the industrial grower leaves the ground bare after the harvest. This reductive behavior allows wind and rain to erode his topsoil, and the silt runoff clogs local streams and rivers.

Worse yet, in the pursuit of illusory efficiency, factory farms tend to overuse both fertilizers and pesticides to ensure a big crop. Some of the excess leaches into the water table and contaminates the groundwater, while some evaporates and creates more acid rain. Whatever is left flows into streams and rivers, polluting drinking water and contributing to huge algae blooms when it reaches the sea. The algae use up all the oxygen in the water, creating hypoxias, or huge dead zones in our oceans where no marine life can exist. One of the world's largest hypoxias is in the Gulf of Mexico, near the mouth of the Mississippi River. Ranging between six and seven thousand square miles in area, it is already larger than Rhode Island and growing rapidly. All told, 146 major hypoxias dot the world's oceans, and all are growing.

Who pays the price for all this contamination, this destruction of the Earth's equity upon which all of us ultimately depend? Not the fertilizer maker or the factory farm per se. It is paid by fishermen and oystermen and scallopers, who can no longer make a living from our contaminated waters. By taxpayers who must bankroll municipal facilities to produce potable water. By people who become ill from drinking tainted water, lose work time, and perhaps incur medical costs. By lumberjacks whose livelihoods are threatened by acid rain–related damage in our forests. In the long run all of us, especially our children, pay a terrible toll for this unnatural approach to "efficiency."

The root cause of all this seems to be that we humans consider our versions of efficiency superior to nature's. This illusion has damaging effects. If you look at farming as a strictly economic enterprise, you virtually guarantee an addiction to oil-based fertilizers and pesticides. Those chemicals inevitably abuse the natural resources on which farming depends. The conventional way of thinking literally turns big farms into excavations—Earth destruction pits—as opposed to verdant cultivation sites that are in harmony with nature's rhythms and systems. The real costs of industrial farming, then, are horrendous, far greater than the ledger entries. Echoing the paradoxical Vietnam-era rationale that we had to destroy a village in order to save it, Big Agribusiness assumes, in effect, that we have to destroy the Earth in order to farm it.

Just as monoculture and factory farming reduce complex biological relationships to easy tricks for soil chemists, so, too, modern industries shrink complex economics to whatever it takes to achieve quick profits at minimum cost. In the name of efficiency, future consequences become irrelevant. Immediate gratification rules. If a job can be done more cheaply elsewhere, it is outsourced; if a supplier can be made to swallow an extra dime of cost, he gets squeezed; if the law allows the emission of X tons of pollutants, factory smokestacks spew out every legal ounce.

The consequences can no longer be ignored. We humans are so careless about our impact on nature that we endanger ourselves, to say nothing of other species. Our own behavior increases the severity of global warming and the resultant droughts, famines, floods, forest fires, and Katrina-scale storms. Millions appear blind to the irony that man, the "rational" animal, keeps trashing the only planet we will ever have.

Business has a special obligation—and opportunity. Given our past depredations in pursuit of profit, companies should now declare war on ecological idiocy. What could be more in our own strategic interest? What could be more genuinely profitable than using business power and know-how to literally save the world?

Most of this case for action was only a hunch that day in 1982 when Kraft's Land Pavilion handed me a mission. I knew that I yearned to help foster a business transformation. But the world is full of hapless prophets. If I wanted to become effective rather than eccentric, I had to somehow create a truly sustainable business that actually made money—and the more, the better.

I began as a small acorn, unlikely to become a mighty oak anytime soon. Realizing that New Alchemy was no business academy, I returned home to New Hampshire and joined Samuel Kaymen, my friend and fellow idealist, in launching what then seemed a pretty quixotic enterprise—Stonyfield Farm, a tiny venture in yogurt production.

Some twenty-five years later, Stonyfield is the world's largest organic-yogurt maker, and I am its CE-Yo. Better yet, our U.S. yogurt sales surpassed those of Kraft's Breyers brand nearly a decade ago. Stonyfield has grown by more than 27 percent a year for the past eighteen straight years, compared with 5 to 7 percent for the yogurt industry as a whole. In 2006, our sales topped $260 million; in 2007, we were on track to exceed $300 million. It's largely due to our focus on sustainability—the art of replacing myopic efficiency with sensible methods that boost profits while benefiting nature rather than destroying it.

High on Stonyfield's agenda is our top priority—real wealth. As a business, we've pledged to do anything feasible to help reduce environmental costs and rebalance the planet's natural systems, from the land to the atmosphere.

In practical terms, we look to nature in striving to make our business as sustainable as possible. Natural examples abound. Consider how a tree builds and supports its own ecosystem. It sprouts leaves that make shade and conserve the water needed for growth. It fertilizes itself by dropping its leaves to the ground, where they decompose into soil that, in turn, nurtures microorganisms needed for the tree's balanced and healthy growth. Certain tree species support epiphytes, such as mosses and bromeliads, that produce nitrogen, another fertilizer for the tree's ecosystem. Many trees also secrete acids that help to break down the soil, thus keeping it friable and absorbent so that life-sustaining moisture can reach the tree's roots. Trees reproduce themselves by sending out seeds, and when stands of trees develop, a windbreak is created, which affords protection to other organisms in the ecosystem. All in all, a tree is an elegant, self-cultivating system devised by nature with no waste.

In essence, the whole Stonyfield story thus far is the learning curve that my co-conspirators and I went through in building a business that defied conventional wisdom. What have I learned? Let's start with the bottom line. It's just this: Sustainability thrives when you open your mind to doing things most businesspeople would consider plain nutty. Examples:

- We pay some of our organic suppliers as much as twice the going rate for conventionally grown materials.
- We do hardly any advertising, and we use our packaging to promote other organizations.
- We actually push for more government oversight and regulation of our industry.
- We give our customers and investors detailed reports on how much pollution and waste we generate—even when those figures are rising.

Our approach is almost diametrically opposed to the ancient business recipe for success: Buy cheap, sell dear. We're willing to spend top dollar to produce the product—and to build the business—that will make us most proud. That's not typical.

Consider the soft-drink industry. The people who make Coke and Pepsi have solidified their empires mostly by always working to reduce the cost of their ingredients. Since 1984, these sugary drinks have contained not a bit of sugar. Pepsi and Coke figured out back then that they could switch to high-fructose corn syrup, save a few cents an ounce, and the consumer wouldn't notice the difference in taste. Next they super-sized the containers and offered twenty-ounce bottles for only pennies more than they used to charge for smaller bottles in the days when they were still using sugar. Gross margins grew tremendously, and they plowed the new revenues into ubiquitous advertising that kept their brands in consumers' faces.

At Stonyfield, however, our goal is more than making money. We aim to be both sustainable and profitable. When we make decisions, we consider the alternatives in terms of whether their impact would move us closer to, or further from, sustainable profitability. Pay more for milk? Yes, if the milk is high-quality and our purchases will ensure long-term access to a key, quality ingredient.

Our unwillingness to manage with only profit in mind seems to work in our favor—even when events play out against us. In 2005, for example, we had to swallow $4 million in unexpected costs because of a shortage of organic milk. We had no choice but to pay our suppliers more than we had planned. To offset the added expense, we had to cut into our already meager marketing budget. Nevertheless, thanks to the loyalty of our customers, we still beat our sales and profit estimates and grew by 25 percent.

Now, I confess that our gross margins are nowhere near that of our competitors'. But here's the beauty part: Our net profit margins are *better* than theirs. At Stonyfield, we turn the old mantra on its head. We buy dear, meaning that we pay top dollar to produce the finest yogurt. And it works for us, just as I know it can work for all companies.

I hasten to acknowledge that I was neither born with this

vision of how to do business, nor bequeathed it by revelation. I certainly had no such idea when I joined Stonyfield Farm in 1983 shortly after its founding. I just muddled along, learning by experience. I deduced that the idea of maximizing gross margins by lowballing the cost of goods, as Coke and Pepsi did, would betray our promise of top-quality yogurt. Honesty was clearly our best policy.

Instead of cheapening the product, we put lots of money into it. Just as we have at times paid almost double the price of nonorganic milk, we also pay more for the rest of our ingredients. We use organic sugar instead of that less expensive high-fructose corn syrup. We don't use modified food starch; we use agar from seaweed extract. We don't use gelatin; we use organic milk solids.

Top-quality ingredients such as these pay off for our customers in higher nutrition and enhanced health benefits, not to mention better taste. It costs significantly more to produce Stonyfield yogurt than, say, Yoplait, our primary competitor. We can't pass all those costs on to the consumer, only some of them. So we had to find a different way to make a profit. In our high-cost, low-margin model, we minimize advertising while assuring customers that they're buying superb yogurt and being part of a planet-saving mission.

And businesses everywhere can do the same.

This book is a catalog of the lessons learned by Stonyfield people seeking profitability via sustainable practices over the past quarter century. I will tell you what works for us, enhancing every chapter of our story with the stories of other companies with similar ambitions.

What's Ahead

In the early days, Samuel and I, both idealists and easily distracted, realized that we might well lose our way as we attempted to cobble up a little yogurt business out of zero resources, unless we created a purpose, a raison d'être to justify the punishment we inflicted on ourselves. This, as I'll explain in chapter 2, led me to compose a Stonyfield mission statement that defined our goals for the first time and has served as our North Star ever since. Simplistic? Not if you're going broke trying to start a business that disdains all business wisdom. We learned that when you're buried in the trenches with your butt under water, a powerful mission statement can—and did—change everything.

From 1995 to 2005, Stonyfield had great success in increasing our efficiency and slashing our carbon dioxide emissions per ton of yogurt we produced. Carbon dioxide emissions contribute to global warming, the gravest environmental threat of our time. Our pollution-cutting efforts, detailed in chapter 3, were equivalent to taking 4,500 cars off the road. Moreover, we saved more than $1.6 million in the process—good reason for all companies to do the same.

In 1997, we were the first manufacturer in the U.S. to mitigate the CO_2 emissions from our facility by investing in carbon offsets—such as reforestation projects and the construction of wind generators.

Another Stonyfield lesson: We couldn't afford advertising, so we came up with inexpensive alternatives that worked even better. One idea was to get known by attracting free press attention for doing outrageous things that amused people without insulting them. Another approach, which I'll discuss in chapter 4, was to forgo all regular ad media and instead use our yogurt cup lids as little billboards for environmental messages that now reach a huge audience—more than 150 million pairs of eyes per year.

Over the years, we've also confirmed that skeptics are right when they say going organic costs more than conventional methods and requires a lot more government regulations. But chapter 5 points out that's actually good news: We found that higher costs and government standards yielded higher profits because they ensure the superior, genuinely organic yogurt that our customers gladly pay more for.

The reason we want our government to validate and defend a strong set of organic standards is that we would like everyone—consumers, farmers, and processors—to know exactly what it means to be organic. The term "natural," for example, has no such standards. There are ice creams on the market that don't change shape when they melt, but they are still labeled "natural." It does no good for either people or nature if organic becomes similarly meaningless, unverifiable, and unenforceable.

Also, I began to see early on that organic is a way of thinking that can help improve any business. By following organic principles, many other industries could become more self-sustaining and thus lessen their destructive impact on our key resources, including air, water, soil, and climate. The Stonyfield record proves they could also boost profits.

Just as we've profited by reducing CO_2 emissions, so we've further reduced Stonyfield's environmental footprint by rethinking waste management. The human tradition, alas, has been to "dilute" garbage by dumping it in the nearest moving water, which takes it to a mythical place called "away," meaning simply out of sight. The new notion of recycling is more enlightened, chapter 6 argues, but only slightly. Had the waste been avoided or reduced in the first place, it would not have to be recycled, with attendant costs for removing and reusing it.

Conversely, we can't ever match nature's ability to waste nothing by reusing everything in closed, self-sustaining systems. We still generate waste, such as tons of yogurt that accumulate from the quality-control process. The strategy that works for us is to sharply reduce certain materials before they begin generating waste. For example, after completing an environmental assessment of our packaging, we eliminated our plastic lid and inner seal in favor of a foil seal, dramatically reducing the amount of packaging material and the energy and water that went into making it. That change alone saved more than $1 million a year.

Here's more: In the United States, at least, all too many companies seem to be at war with their suppliers, forcing them to slash prices and then skimp on quality just to stay alive. We learned early on that organic farming enriches soil and cows, thus producing better milk, and we set about helping our organic dairymen to cash in as well. Freeing them from the crazy month to month price swings that afflict other milk suppliers, we have brought stability to our organic milk producers by committing to consistent prices disconnected from the roller-coaster ups and downs of the commodity milk market. Moreover, as I discuss in chapter 7, we've applied the same principle of stable, fair pricing to the worldwide suppliers of all other ingredients we need, such as berries, cocoa, and sugar. Everyone benefits.

Whatever the variations from one business to the next, some twenty-five years of hard-won success at Stonyfield tell me that sustainability is the correct grail for business leaders to pursue in the early twenty-first century. Those who do will reap unimagined rewards for themselves and the planet—a vision of which I share in chapter 8. This is no longer a hypothesis; it's a surefire plan for solid transformation. I could sit down with anyone at any level of a company, walk through his or her business, and come up with numerous alternative choices that could make the business more sustainable and more profitable.

There's another incentive to pursue sustainability—self-defense. In a fast-approaching era of global warming and climate consciousness, more government regulations are as inevitable as the environmental accidents, cleanups, and lawsuits that will saddle complacent industries with heavy burdens of proof. The survivors are sure to be those who see the future and agilely join the vanguard, embracing sustainability and other reforms geared to the world as it is, not as they might wish it to be. From those survivors will come the next generation's winners, the players who adapt to new realities best and fastest.

Some business leaders already get it. Take Dow Chemical's former CEO, Bill Stavropoulos. Bill and I were on a national town meeting panel on sustainability some time back, and the moderator, a *BusinessWeek* editor, threw me a curveball. "Gary, you're into organic agriculture, meaning you're against pesticides," he said. "The CEO of Dow is in the pesticide business.

Is one of you wrong?" I shot back, "Yes, he's wrong." I got a spontaneous standing ovation.

Then I added a twist on my original Epcot epiphany. "But I envy Bill's position," I said, explaining that he could probably do more for my children and grandchildren with one purchase order than I could do in my entire career. With his power, he could change the world.

Not long after, I spoke at another meeting where Bill was also on the program. He insisted that I go first. When he stood up, he displayed two potential Dow products, a T-shirt made from organic cotton and a yogurt cup made from corn. "This is the future," he told the audience. Then it was his turn to get an ovation, and I was one of the people applauding.

As Bob Dylan sang, "The times they are a-changin'."

For me, it's been a long journey from youthful naïveté to aging clarity, but every step, however difficult, has given me the pleasure of discovering how nature's wisdom can become humankind's salvation. Now comes my greatest pleasure: I am sharing all I've learned, and you are reading these words. Please keep reading. There's much to share—and much to gain.

2

Mission Control

By 1982, my life at the New Alchemy Institute had become very stressful. I was supposed to raise $750,000 each year, a nearly impossible feat after Ronald Reagan became president. Not only did the Reaganites immediately slash funding for federal environmental projects, but their policies effectively drained away private money from programs like ours. And the new administration also abolished tax incentives that encouraged Americans to invest in solar power and other sustainable energy sources. Green was no longer fashionable.

President Reagan's very first executive order, literally signed on Inauguration Day, abolished the Community Services Administration (CSA), a federal agency that supported local activists trying to help poor people. The Cape and Islands Self-Reliance Corporation, a nonprofit energy-conservation group that I had helped found, landed the last grant in CSA history, thanks to an outgoing director, Dick Saul, who shepherded our request to approval and made sure we got our money.

We planned to spend a fruitful year weatherizing affordable housing and setting up year-round organic gardens. All we needed to make it happen was the grant money. Most of Dick's department had already resigned by the eve of the inauguration, so he personally carried our check to the post office. We received it postmarked 11:30 A.M. on January 20, 1981, and wasted no time in cashing it. Reagan was sworn in at 12:01 P.M. Less than half an hour later, the CSA was gone, a victim of conservative politics.

Even though New Alchemy depended on very few federal dollars for its survival, the Reagan cutbacks mortally wounded us by drying up the private contributions we counted on for support. Charitable foundations like the Rockefeller Brothers Fund were so inundated with new pleas for cash that they simply raised a white flag and quit giving to most of their prior applicants. It was all they could do to provide emergency funding for programs dealing with truly urgent situations. Issues like energy conservation and organic farming took a backseat.

Clearly, it was time for me to make a change. If I launched a successful business, I thought, I could use some of its profits to support and promote environmental causes. But of all the forms this supposed bonanza might take—and my head teemed with possibilities—none was more improbable than the one I stumbled into when I joined forces with a self-taught yogurt-making genius from Brooklyn, New York.

Samuel Kaymen, one of the most focused men I've ever known, was a brilliant former defense-industry engineer in search of a higher purpose. Having met Samuel and his wife, Louise, a few years earlier, I knew he had switched lifestyle gears twice, first to become a hippie and then to found The Rural

Education Center, an organic farming school in Wilton, New Hampshire. Now a lively graybeard with twinkling blue eyes, Samuel was a man of imperfections as endearing as they were maddening. He had the penetrating mind of a superb engineer but not a single business corpuscle anywhere in his body. His organic farming center was virtually bankrupt, on the brink of being plowed under.

At that troubling moment, hoping to help save the center, I agreed to become a trustee. I loved the concept of sustainable farming with its inherent affinity with and respect for nature, so unlike business as I knew it then. I particularly admired Samuel's ambition to help farmers stabilize their shaky finances and gain the secure lives they deserved. We were kindred spirits.

As a trustee, I first concentrated on new ideas to meet the center's $150,000 annual budget. But equally urgent was the need to help focus Samuel and his assistant director, Grace Gershuny, on priorities. They were seat-of-the-pants managers, and both were completely overcommitted and overwhelmed. They spent their days sprinkling water on small brush fires while ignoring the inferno erupting at their backs. When I added up Samuel's weekly commitments, he was scheduled for a whopping 156 hours. I convinced him to eliminate unnecessary activities and put his laserlike brain to work on two fronts: fulfilling the center's mission and generating revenues. That's how we came to zero in on the yogurt business.

Samuel was already an astute maker of yogurt, which he described as the perfect food. In fact, he had gone back to Brooklyn to talk to some Orthodox Jewish guys he knew who made yogurt in their back rooms. They divulged their secret: "It's the *vetha*," they explained in their heavily accented English, meaning that great yogurt depends on great weather—a perfect blend of temperatures and timing. After much trial and error, Samuel had cracked the *vetha* code for himself, learning how to tune the process to suit the thermometer and humidity. Certain that he had a unique product, he became an impassioned dairyman, milking his farm's cows and selling yogurt under the Stonyfield label through The Rural Education Center.

But Samuel owed $35,000 he couldn't pay back, and he was slipping further behind every day. He couldn't pay rent or salaries. He had no capital whatsoever. Exhausted and financially strapped, he asked me to come aboard full-time.

I loved Samuel, a compelling eccentric on a holy mission. I loved his yogurt, the most delicious I'd ever tasted. And I loved the hills of my native New Hampshire. How could I not agree to help run his business?

The day I arrived, September 15, 1983, I opened the door to the office and found three Army surplus desks piled chest-high with teetering stacks of unpaid bills. I looked for the bank deposits to balance out the bills. There were none—Samuel had cashed every incoming check to buy feed and supplies. By 3:30 that afternoon, after opening every envelope, I'd calculated that we were $75,000 in the red. The electricity was about to be cut off. Stonyfield Farm was a beautiful dream created by a beautiful guy. It was also virtually dead on my arrival.

So I did the only thing possible in that situation: I called my mother and borrowed $30,000. Then I called other friends, family members, and Stonyfield trustees and managed to raise another $45,000 to gain some breathing room. Finally, I called our landlord, Tony Blair, and told him we couldn't pay the rent—gulp—for the next year. Although he was far from happy about the situation, he agreed to accept my vague promise for some kind of ultimate payback in lieu of rent. It was a decision that would eventually result in a financial windfall for him, but none of us could have predicted that at this precarious moment.

My reward for all this was a demanding new life that entailed chores like helping Samuel milk the cows twice each day and make yogurt every weekend, often in subfreezing weather. But we toiled on, increasingly aware that we needed to be totally clear about why we were beating ourselves up like this—not for self-affirmation alone, but also to spread our environmental gospel and convince others to join in our cause.

We had started with vats of yogurt and a fuzzy notion of making money by persuading the world that our products could help clean up the planet and save family farmers. But we had never refined our ideas. Every world-saving (and money-making) business needs a stated mission—a rallying cry that focuses efforts, helps set priorities, and gives all hands a meaning and a purpose. So one night I sat down with a bottle of cabernet and wrote a mission statement that has barely changed since. Stonyfield is in business:

- To provide the very highest-quality, best-tasting, all-natural, and certified organic products.
- To educate consumers and producers about the value of protecting the environment and supporting family farmers and sustainable farming methods.
- To serve as a model that environmentally and socially responsible businesses can also be profitable.

- To provide a healthful, productive, and enjoyable workplace for all employees, with opportunities to gain new skills and advance personal career goals.
- To recognize our obligations to stockholders and lenders by providing an excellent return on their investment.

The next morning at breakfast, I showed Samuel and Louise what I had written. It was, after all, still their company, and I valued their opinions. They didn't change a word. So now we had a mission statement. All we needed was a viable business to go with it.

After twenty-five years, I am glad to report that the mission I backed into has produced a successful company that combines profitable business with a powerful purpose. The truth is, even I had doubts back in 1983 that Stonyfield Farm could reject conventional business wisdom, however perverse we judged it to be, and still prosper financially. Our decision was basically a gamble that a truly honest product—pure yogurt—would attract customers so in tune with our environmental goals that both our business and our ideals would flourish. The gamble paid off, but only after we made our mission clear to ourselves, our customers, our investors, and the world.

A Good Soul Is Your Best Asset

H. L. Mencken once said that to every complex problem, there is an answer that is easy, simple, and wrong. Similarly, even the clearest mission statement can be the wrong one. After all, business is full of highly purposeful companies that leave the world in worse shape. Consider the mission statement that Exxon (now ExxonMobil) operated under in 1989. The company's mission was brutally clear: "To provide our shareholders with a superior return on investment." Nothing else mattered. And Exxon's reaction was true to that mission when its oil tanker *Exxon Valdez* went aground, spilling 11 million gallons of fuel oil in Alaska's Prince Edward Sound.

The spill fouled some fifteen hundred miles of Alaskan shoreline, destroying fishing grounds and leaving otters, seals, seabirds, bald eagles, salmon, and whales coated with oily slime that doomed thousands to premature death. Yet Exxon professed itself immune to any obligation beyond the almighty return on the investor's dollar. Ten days after the disaster, it paid $1.8 million for advertisements in 166 U.S. newspapers, apologizing for the spill but accepting no responsibility. Ultimately, the cleanup would cost the company more than $2.5 billion, as well as its reputation.

At the time, though, the only consequence Exxon cared about was a public-relations meltdown, which it handled by rewriting its mission statement and adding some bromides about ethical standards and environmental responsibilities. Anyone can detect the seriousness of the fix from ExxonMobil's subsequent decision to become a major backer of the Competitive Enterprise Institute, which argues that global warming is not a problem worth fussing about. One of the group's commercials claims that too much CO_2 is a good thing. "They call it pollution," the tagline reads. "We call it life."

In effect, the ExxonMobil mission statement has not changed since the oil spill, when it reflected a failure of corporate imagination, or arrested development, or both. Painful as it may be for a Fortune 100 company, the truth is that Exxon-Mobil talked big and thought small.

A more benign but no less painful variation on that theme is the company with two contradictory missions. One is the chief executive's high-minded call for ecological sanity, the other an insatiable appetite for profits at whatever cost. This disconnect isn't necessarily sinister, just a dumb dichotomy waiting for disaster. Consider the embarrassing case of BP's former chief executive officer, John Browne. Long an eloquent friend of the environment, Sir John backed up his words with an $8 billion scheme to develop alternative energies. But despite his greenspeak, money talked louder inside BP's culture, and penny-pinching trumped both safety and the ecology. Twin setbacks erupted—a deadly refinery explosion in Texas and an ecologically damaging leak in one of BP's pipelines on Alaska's North Slope. Huge fines for safety violations ensued, driving down BP's stock price and accelerating Sir John's early retirement.

Ford Motor also specialized in double-talk. Former CEO William Clay Ford, Jr., was a well-known figure in environmental circles, funding conservation initiatives with his own millions and spending billions of the company's cash to overhaul the automaker's huge and polluting River Rouge plant. Meanwhile, Ford assembly lines tirelessly contradicted his rhetoric. Off rolled thousands of gas-guzzling SUVs and pickup trucks, all flawlessly equipped to worsen global warming.

Caught between skeptical directors and demanding stockholders, many CEOs become environmentalists in word only. They apparently don't have the clout, or perhaps the stomach, to butt up against their organizations' time-honored money-making propositions. The mission is a myth.

But this is no cause for giving up on corporate allies. Whatever its internal confusions, I believe, every consumer products company has enormous educational potential. It's just a question of what you want to teach and how seriously you want to take it. I see no reason why General Electric can't educate people about energy efficiency, or, for that matter, why Ford can't educate people about fuel economy, and why ExxonMobil and BP can't lead the masses toward renewable energy. Skeptics will say I'm being naïve: Public companies have no interest in saving the world; they're all about enriching shareholders, period. To which I reply: That's shortsighted and ultimately self-defeating. A company that appeals to the customer's best instincts while delivering high-quality products has a competitive edge that today's sophisticated consumers find irresistible. Serving humanity pays.

Just in the past couple of years, that truth has become evident to some of the biggest and most influential companies in the world. Corporate giants including IBM and DuPont are moving to curb their emissions; such food processors as Frito-Lay, Kellogg's, and Heinz now offer organic products and entire organic brand lines. Wal-Mart—not only America's biggest retailer, but the world's largest company—has made the commitment to sustainability in all its practices and operations. And in 2007, Rupert Murdoch announced that his News Corporation, a media giant that spans the globe, will become carbon-neutral in three short years. He promised that messages about climate change will be woven into the content of all his news and entertainment outlets, and predicted—accurately, I'm sure—that even his most conservative zealots, Sean Hannity and Bill O'Reilly, will get the message.

Murdoch said he had been converted to an activist on the global warming issue by talks with his son James and by the impact of a three-year drought in his native Australia. But his zeal is backed up by shrewd practicality. "Acting on this issue is simply good business," he said. Whatever it costs to make News Corp. sustainable, he predicted, will be more than made up by increased efficiency, better morale among employees, and the added loyalty of younger viewers and readers who are already backing environmental causes.

I applaud Rupert Murdoch's business sense. In the end, whatever the size of your enterprise, if your mission statement sets clear and inspiring expectations, and if you truly make it the cornerstone of your operations—your unique and enduring reason for being—you will have no trouble convincing customers of the superiority of your products and services. Your honesty will be your calling card.

With these specs in mind, let's reconsider Stonyfield's mission statement as a prototype for any business. It consists of five sub-missions listed in strategic order:

- *Mission 1:* The company will sell only superior products, the prerequisite for becoming a market contender and a rallying point for employees to maintain top quality. Merely acceptable products will be unacceptable. There is no business future in mediocrity.
- *Mission 2:* The company will use its products and services to educate people about a cause they care about. A lot of

people don't trust companies. Having a worthy mission suggests that an organization is different. It says that the people behind this product are caring human beings with a good purpose. At the very least, we all prefer to buy from friendly, considerate people rather than robots or remote executives. Our competitor Yoplait, for example, has done a wonderful job supporting the fight against breast cancer.

- *Mission 3:* The company will prove that a cause-driven enterprise can also succeed as a business. Achieving this double feature may sound harder than it is. In fact, the mission can provide the extra clout to defeat competitors, because a strong mission makes your business better. Missions are also powerful marketing tools. The fact that Paul Newman makes a line of tasty salad dressings (Newman's Own) is a ho-hum story worth two sentences in a gossip column. The fact that he donates 100 percent of his company's profits to charity is a great story that warms hearts everywhere. By no coincidence, half gallons of Newman's Own lemonade fly off grocery shelves in all fifty states.
- *Mission 4:* The company will deliver on its mission privately as well as publicly. It respects every person's desire for meaningful work, for jobs that have a higher purpose than money alone. Missions also help to attract and retain superb colleagues. The company believes that a humane mission telegraphs its determination to do business in ways that unify all employees as committed stakeholders, both morally and financially.
- *Mission 5:* The company is fully committed to providing stockholders with the best possible return on their

> investments. Profits are neither wrong nor immoral, and doing business the sustainable way pays dividends to both investors and the environment. In fact, the company believes that its parallel commitment to human values will actually enhance its financial performance rather than impede it. All evidence thus far shows that a company with an appealing mission is likely to outperform its profits-only rivals in nearly any market. As the subtitle above notes, a good soul is your best asset.

Stonyfield, of course, is in no way unique in parlaying a planet-friendly mission into rising sales and profits. Here are the stories of four companies best known for remarkable fidelity to the ecological missions that have driven them to fame and fortune.

Patagonia: The Home of Eco-Warriors

My own enthusiasm for sustainable enterprise is given extra weight by the achievements of others. One need look no further than Patagonia, the California-based outdoor equipment maker founded forty years ago by Yvon Chouinard. Though he calls himself "the reluctant businessman," Chouinard has scaled the heights of commerce as nimbly as he once climbed sheer rock faces from the Alps to the Rockies. The man has impeccable business instincts. He chose the name Patagonia, for example, because it evokes "romantic visions of glaciers tumbling into fjords, jagged windswept peaks, gauchos, and condors." It also has a lovely ring, and can be pronounced in every language.

Patagonia, the company, emphasizes simplicity, utility, and a deep-seated concern for the environment in the clothing and gear it designs for skiers, snowboarders, surfers, fly casters, paddlers, trail runners, and, of course, climbers. But what makes the enterprise work exceptionally well is its mission: "To make the best product, cause no unnecessary harm, and use business to inspire and implement solutions to the environmental crisis." That compact statement has galvanized Patagonia's more than twelve hundred employees to keep the company growing at an admirable clip, while maintaining an enviable reputation for quality and an awareness of its environmental impact that are second to none.

Not surprisingly for a company that views sustainability as its top priority, Patagonia puts its money where its mission is, annually donating to environmental groups the larger of 10 percent of profits or 1 percent of sales. Yvon Chouinard calls the self-imposed assessment his "Earth tax," a sum he feels is owed for being a polluter and a user of the planet's nonrenewable resources. In his view, if we wait for the government to live up to its responsibilities and impose such a tax, the Earth will be totally beyond repair. His words and ideas have struck a chord with other concerned businessmen and women; 728 organizations have, as of August 2007, joined an alliance called 1% for the Planet. But that's not good enough. Like me, Chouinard wants to convince other companies that doing right by the planet is a viable and more profitable way of doing business.

Chouinard, now in his late sixties, began climbing as a teenager in Southern California in the mid-1950s. Progressing to the big walls farther north in Yosemite National Park, he was soon troubled by the then-common practice of climbers leaving behind the soft-iron pitons used to secure ropes while ascending a mountain face. Too soft to be removed easily, the pitons remained embedded in the rock, a kind of littering that Chouinard considered unseemly and damaging to the cliffs. He decided to make his own reusable pitons from harder stuff that could be easily removed when the climb was finished. He bought a coal-fired forge, tongs, an anvil, and a hammer and began to teach himself blacksmithing.

After Chouinard and a friend tried out his first creations on Yosemite rock, word began to get around. Soon, all their climbing buddies wanted the reusable chrome-molybdenum steel pitons. So the fledgling blacksmith began to forge a business out of hammered bits of steel that he sold from the back of his car for $1.50 each. Traveling between climbing venues and barely supporting himself on what he earned from his portable forge, Chouinard had to supplement his meager store-bought provisions with such delicacies as ground squirrel and porcupine. But hang on he did, until word of mouth finally widened demand for his gear. In 1965, he formed a partnership with his climbing friend Tom Frost, and switched from handmade to machine-made products marketed under the Chouinard Equipment brand.

The growing popularity of rock climbing in the 1960s was both a blessing and a curse for the environmentally conscious Chouinard and Frost. While ramped-up sales of climbing gear were making their company successful, the repeated hammering in and taking out of pitons was disfiguring the fragile rock on well-traveled routes. What to do? The pair decided to stop making and using their mainstay product, the steel pitons—a move many would call stupid, if not downright suicidal, from a business point of view. To Chouinard and Frost, however, continuing to scar Mother Nature's beautiful face was not an option.

Chouinard Equipment found economic daylight in aluminum chocks, which could be wedged by hand rather than hammered in and out of the cracks in the rock face. Thanks to articles in the company's equipment catalog explaining the hazards of pitons and the joys of "clean climbing" with the new aluminum product, the chocks were soon selling faster than Chouinard Equipment could make them. It wouldn't be the last time that Chouinard's profits went up when the company sided with the environment, confirming his belief that "profit is what happens when you do everything else right."

Around that time in the early 1970s, Yvon also discovered the nearly indestructible regulation rugby shirt while on a climbing trip in Scotland. He thought it far better for his rigorous sport than the then-standard one. When friends back home saw him wearing the heavyweight blue-cotton pullover with red and yellow stripes, they all wanted one. Chouinard Equipment tried to oblige by importing the colorful shirts from Australia, England, and New Zealand, setting in motion a sea change in men's outdoor clothing, which, up until that time, had been limited to basic drab.

The popularity of the shirts encouraged the company to supplement its modestly profitable hardware business with other apparel—gloves, hats, raingear, and such—which, in turn, led to the adoption of a new name, Patagonia. The idea was to associate the company with a faraway Eden of untouched ecosystems that a rugged outdoorsy type might dream of inhabiting. It worked. Used at first only for the clothing line, Patagonia became the name on the company door in 1989, when it set up a world headquarters in Ventura, California.

From its initial decision to scrap steel pitons and put environmental sustainability ahead of traditional business logic, Patagonia has evolved into a global cheerleader for the planet, a role that consumers and employees alike have responded to with gusto. It runs major campaigns to focus attention on issues ranging from the removal of dams to protect endangered fish to the harm unfettered globalization of trade can pose to the environment. Patagonia donates substantial time and money—$27 million over the past two decades—to small groups working to save or restore natural habitats, preferring grassroots efforts over bigger operations that typically come with big staffs, big overhead, and ties to big corporations. And it runs "Tools for Activists" conferences to show the groups it sponsors how best to use marketing and public relations skills in their battles against air and water pollution, global warming, deforestation, acid rain, and all the other man-made threats to life on this planet.

Patagonia's bias toward small, local efforts was forged in the 1970s, after employees helped fight and win a nearby battle to save what was left of the degraded Ventura River habitat, once a major steelhead-salmon spawning ground. After development plans were defeated and cleanup projects undertaken, the supposedly "dead" river miraculously came back to life. Wildlife, including the steelhead, returned and prospered.

The realization that significant results could be achieved by just a handful of dedicated, energetic people convinced Chouinard to focus his resources on arming a multitude of small groups to do battle in hundreds if not thousands of trouble spots around the world. You start thinking locally, he says, and before long you realize that "it's a small planet and we've got to save all of it."

Patagonia's latest endeavor is rehabilitating the San Elijo Lagoon in Cardiff-by-the-Sea, California, where, in June of 2006, the company opened its first surf-focused gear and apparel shop. Like everything else Patagonian, the shop is Earth-friendly, from the materials used in the store itself—reclaimed wood, recycled steel fixtures, and paint free of volatile organic compounds—to the fabrics and dyes used in its clothes.

Patagonia has long realized that lending support to other activists is only one part of the environmental equation. Reducing its own role as a corporate polluter is the other. To that end, Patagonia bans paper cups and plastic trash-can liners from its offices, and uses recycled paper in its catalogs, recycled lumber, rebar, and carpet in its buildings, and recycled plastic from soda bottles in its fleece clothing line. In one of its latest industry-leading efforts, it is even recycling some of its old fabrics to make new ones.

With ads trumpeting "We want your underwear," Patagonia launched its Common Threads program to get customers to send in their worn-out pieces of polyester long underwear (preferably laundered) for use in making new polyester undergarments. Besides saving space in overburdened landfills, Patagonia estimates that recycling, compared to making new polyester fiber, reduces energy use by 76 percent and CO_2 emissions by 71 percent.

The company has also retrofitted lighting systems in existing stores to make them more energy-efficient, and it cut energy use by 60 percent in its Reno, Nevada, distribution center through the installation of radiant heating and solar-tracking skylights that capture more of the sun's usable light. Scraps from its corporate cafeteria go into the company's compost heap, and diaper-changing tables at its day-care center are covered with used computer paper.

A decade ago, Patagonia eliminated fabric colors made from components most toxic to the environment, and about the same time it embarked on a crusade that has prompted big apparel makers including Nike and Gap Inc. to rethink their own use of materials. After its research showed that "natural" cotton grown the usual agribusiness way is a huge source of toxic pesticides in our soil and water, Patagonia decided in 1996 to make a total switch to cotton that was certified 100 percent organic.

It took a Herculean effort to find enough farmers who could supply organic cotton to make the amount of fabric Patagonia needed, and to locate ginners and spinners who would agree to rid their equipment of pesticide residue for what was considered a small product run. Patagonia also had to make sure that every fiber could be traced back to a particular bale so that they could be assured that it was indeed organic. Within a short eighteen months, the company succeeded in changing the cotton content of sixty-six of its products to 100 percent organic.

As these efforts demonstrate, the company never rests in its battle to find better, more Earth-friendly products and the ways and means of producing them. Simple design and superb finishing are guiding principles, but, again, the company's top priority is the planet's well-being. If anything, conventional business practices and the profits they produce are openly shunned. Yvon Chouinard has made saving the world his primary mission. And that, it seems, is a big part of the company's charm in the eyes of both employees and customers.

But Patagonia also offers a cautionary tale, a reminder that excess in any crusade, not excepting planetary salvation, is apt to inflate the pride that goeth before a fall. In 1991, a recession hit the company hard. Sales went flat, profits crumbled, and the company's bank pulled in its line of credit. Lulled by its previously rapid growth, Patagonia dawdled as inventory piled up and then had to be sold off at a loss. Worst of all, an organization known for taking care of its employees was forced to lay off 120 people, or 20 percent of its workforce, a day that Yvon Chouinard calls "the single darkest day in the company's history."

But Yvon embraced a philosophic, almost grateful tone in describing the disaster: "We were on a suicide course," he told a writer at *Inc.* magazine in 1992, "exceeding our limits, financially and mentally." The company came close to losing its independence. Even so, the crisis actually helped get Patagonia to resume its mission, teaching Yvon and other managers a valuable lesson: Keep growth and borrowing modest and manageable. Today, the company aims for steady growth of about 5 percent a year, a healthy pace that it exceeded by two percentage points in 2005.

During the 1991 crisis, some analysts predicted that the downturn would force Yvon to sacrifice his unorthodox mission and "stifling eco-orthodoxy" in favor of getting a better grip on manufacturing and distribution. To the critics' chagrin, Patagonia's guiding light was not remotely dimmed. Staying firmly on message, Yvon was able to right the company without shelving any of the cultural values he and the company live by.

Employees are still encouraged to grab their boards and head for the beach when the surf's up. Performance expectations remain high, and the work always has to get done, but flextime at Patagonia stretches well beyond family emergencies. Patagonians can be found playing volleyball in the company sandpit and eating healthy, mostly vegetarian meals in the company cafeteria. All hands, even part-timers, get medical benefits, and parents are encouraged to bring their children to the on-site care center, one of the first in the country when it was established at the insistence of Malinda Chouinard, Yvon's wife and business partner. The company, by the way, regularly makes the lists of best places to work in America.

As for that supposedly "stifling eco-orthodoxy" that permeates the company, Chouinard's dogma appears to be swelling, not thinning, the ranks of those clamoring for a seat among the Patagonia faithful. An average of nine hundred people apply for every job the company advertises, even though it pays only the going rate or just barely more. That's the power of a mission, as is the loyalty Patagonia employees feel for the man who inspires them. "Yvon got so much respect in the company that people would listen to him over the professional managers," one of those managers complained to a reporter.

Just recently, three professional surfers who came on board to help run Patagonia's new surf business mimicked that attitude when they professed no regrets about taking big pay cuts. More important was their discovery that they and Yvon shared concerns over water pollution and the wastefulness that threatens sustainability. Those involved in the surfing project agree that a lot of their current products are toxic to the environment—from the materials and processes used in printing the magazines and books chronicling the sport, to the wetsuits, T-shirts, and fins the surfers wear, right down to the boards they mount to catch a wave. Patagonia is working to create a totally "green" board and to give surfing the environmental footprint it currently lacks—and surfers love it.

Meanwhile, Yvon himself continues to embody the spirit of Patagonia's mission when he practices his "MBA" style of management. That means "management by absence," as Yvon takes extended vacations from the office to fish for steelhead salmon in icy Canadian waters and bonefish off Christmas Island in the Indian Ocean, or to climb a glacier on Mount Kenya. Not the least bit apologetic, Yvon points out that his out-of-office activities help the business by spawning new product ideas and giving him the chance to test the quality of those products it already markets.

When the boss is in, however, he's totally focused on the job at hand. In fact, I would dispute his characterization of himself as a reluctant businessman, because you simply don't make money by being reluctant. You make money by enforcing exacting standards, putting your heart and soul into producing the best possible product, and, above all, holding fiercely to your mission.

Is the man unorthodox? Absolutely. But like me, Yvon followed an unplanned entrepreneurial route that evolved in a wholly logical fashion. Both of us started with a recognized need, and both of us came to understand that the power and profits we gained could be directed toward a powerful mission—ours was saving the Earth. The bonus we enjoy is neatly summed up by Yvon when he says that he's "never made an environmental decision that hasn't turned out to be profitable."

The numbers back him up. From just $2 million in 1978, Patagonia's sales multiplied many times over to reach $275 million in 2006, while operating margins run at the high end of the industry's 8 to 12 percent average—and that's after giving away 1 percent of revenues to save a planet that even critics would have to admit they can't live without. The late environmentalist David Brower put it best when he said: "There's no business to be done on a dead planet."

Whole Foods: Working for a Mission, Not Money

There's always been a whiff of unorthodoxy about Whole Foods. It opened for business in Austin, Texas, in 1980, after founder John Mackey moved his Safer Way Natural Foods from his garage to a more Bohemian neighborhood and merged it with another local health-food store. One of only a handful of natural and organic supermarkets in those days, Mackey's fledgling venture grew from a staff of nineteen people to more than thirty-nine thousand team members, who today staff counters bulging with fresh seafood, meat and poultry, baked goods, cheese, produce, and prepared foods, surrounded by shelves of natural and organic body-care preparations, pet products, and assorted household items. The company's 192 stores boasted total sales of $5.6 billion and profits of $203.8 million in 2006. Granted, its stock price has declined from its peak, but I'm not the least bit concerned—and I speak as a shareholder. As often happens, Wall Street is punishing the company for pioneering a business model that its competitors are now embracing. To put it another way, Whole Foods was at the center of a financial bubble that one day had to burst, but it remains one of the strongest and most impressive businesses I know.

How has Whole Foods fulfilled its mission and achieved so much? By acting like anything but a traditional grocer. Its Declaration of Interdependence states: "We go to extraordinary lengths to satisfy and delight our customers." And that's no lie. Putting a new twist on the old saying that the customer is always right, customers at Whole Foods are "not people to argue or match wits with . . . [but] fellow human beings with feelings and emotions . . . equals to be treated with courtesy and respect." Such valued individuals quite naturally deserve, and thus are treated to, an inviting cornucopia of delightful sights and smells—from the palette of gorgeous colors on display in Whole Foods' fresh produce section to the enticing aromas wafting from its baked goods department, which happen to perfectly complement the scent of freshly ground and brewed organic coffee beans.

But because the company sells only natural and organic foods, even quality is defined somewhat differently. Whenever possible, produce is free of pesticides, artificial colorings, and preservatives. Meats come from hormone- and antibiotic-free animals, while the seafood buyers avoid mercury, PCBs, and antibiotics. Customers are encouraged to think of Whole Foods as the place to shop for the best ingredients for a healthy lifestyle.

For team members who make the Whole Foods mission a reality, the rewards extend from fully paid health benefits to a stock-option program geared toward the lower and middle rungs of the ladder, not the top. Team members determine their own benefits packages in a company-wide vote taken every three years, and salaries are linked to performance. However, unlike most companies, Whole Foods allows anyone to find out what another team member, including an executive, makes by looking in the "salary book."

Whole Foods regularly appears on *Fortune*'s list of best places to work, moving up to the number five spot in 2007. The company attributes its culture of empowerment to team members' favorable view of their company. (Two-thirds of the *Fortune* scoring system depends on employee responses to survey questions related to job satisfaction, management attitudes, and company camaraderie.) At Whole Foods, hierarchy gives way to leader-led teams of employees who have a real say in what goes on, participating in decisions about who gets hired and fired. Rule-breaking in service of the company's mission is actively encouraged.

In support of its environmental commitment, Whole Foods Market recently added an innovative product: the Wind Power Card. Now shoppers at eighty Whole Foods stores in eight states can show their support for renewable energy by purchasing wind energy credits at the checkout counter. The credits offset a consumer's monthly electricity use by sending clean, renewable wind energy to the power grid in place of an equivalent amount of fossil-fuel-produced power. In 2006, Whole Foods was the largest nongovernmental buyer of wind energy credits (RECs is what they are officially called) in North America, and the first Fortune 500 company to offset all of its electricity use with wind energy credits. Whole Foods also takes advantage of solar power and power generated by biomass at several of its stores. Sometime in mid-2007, Wells Fargo increased their RECs (but not to 100 percent), followed by Pepsico (and theirs was 100 percent).

A long list of its other mission-driven initiatives ranges from green building with recycled and renewable materials to in-store composting and recycling programs. The company stocks its dining areas with reusable and/or biodegradable dinnerware, uses soy inks for its printed materials, supports carpooling and public transportation use by employees, and works with its suppliers to eliminate Styrofoam packaging and shipping materials.

Whole Foods indirectly reduces environmental damage through its Whole Planet Foundation, which fights poverty by providing educational programs and credit opportunities for struggling populations in third world countries.

Global in nature, the Whole Foods mission is advanced by the company's commitment to making positive choices for the environment and the communities in which it operates. By operating in such admirable fashion, Whole Foods Market proves that it is great missions that make great companies.

New Belgium: A Brewer for the Planet

Any entrepreneur who names his leading product after an old cruiser bike probably has a natural penchant for environmental causes, I figured, when I started hearing about an up-and-coming specialty brewer in Colorado. I figured right. Jeff Lebesch, cofounder of New Belgium Brewing in Fort Collins, cares a lot about making excellent beer and ale with unusual ingredients such as lemon verbena, coriander, and kaffir lime leaves. He also cares about creating a mythology and an ethos around his brews, one that helps his products market themselves. But he cares just as much—maybe more—about doing it all sustainably.

Known primarily for its whimsically branded Fat Tire Amber Ale (named after the mid-1980s bike trip in which Jeff fell in love with Belgian beers and their creative ingredients), New Belgium has excelled at promoting beer as part of an active but laid-back lifestyle. The brewery also has worked hard to incorporate social responsibility in all it does, and to brand itself as an environmental steward.

It's not just talk. Indeed, most industry observers think Jeff worked harder than anybody in the brewing industry to achieve true carbon reduction and sustainability—anybody, that is, except his wife, Kim Jordan. She's been the CEO of the company since 2000, when Jeff kicked himself upstairs to the board of directors. He, a former electrical engineer, has a penchant for tinkering on the technical side. She, a former social worker, puts the community-oriented impetus behind the effort and builds employee support for it. It's a pairing as powerful as a Fat Tire Amber Ale in what the brewery calls a "worthy" glass, alongside a plate of grilled salmon.

Let me set the table for what Jeff and Kim have accomplished, environmentally speaking, since founding the company in their basement a mere sixteen years ago: This brewing operation's electrical energy needs have been 100 percent wind-powered since 1999, making it the first brewery in the nation to eschew the use of fossil fuels. This switch to wind power saved 20 million pounds of coal and prevented the release of 28 million pounds of CO_2 into the atmosphere—in just the first three years of operation.

In addition, New Belgium makes electric power from its wastewater-treatment operation. In a cogeneration process that utilizes the methane that is released while cleaning the wastewater, New Belgium produces up to 20 percent of the electricity it uses. But New Belgium isn't just conserving on the supply side; it is also able to recapture the heat waste from this process to offset some of its thermal energy needs. On the demand side, the brewery also has a "Merlin" brew that is 65 percent more efficient than a traditional brewhouse kettle. They use heat exchangers wherever possible to cut the amount of energy they need. The brewery also employs timers and motion detectors to turn lights on and off and has installed light shelves in many office areas. For the holidays last year, Jeff and Kim gave each of their coworkers five compact fluorescent lightbulbs—along with a profit-sharing check.

These carbon accomplishments are all the more remarkable when you take stock of New Belgium from a strictly business perspective. Jeff and Kim have succeeded in pursuing sustainable business practices while also building one heck of a strong company. Though New Belgium distributes its products in only sixteen western states, it ranks higher in sales volume than many specialty brewers that sell nationwide. According to the Beer Marketers Insights Web site, New Belgium's production ranked third among specialty breweries in 2006, and its growth rate has been consistently in double-digits for more than five years. Being privately held, New Belgium does not report its profits. But certainly this is a healthy enterprise.

Like Stonyfield, New Belgium pays more to do things right. At a 2.5-cent premium per kilowatt hour, or about 30 percent more than the cost of coal-generated electricity, it may never truly "pay" in financial accounting terms for New Belgium to have chosen wind power. Yet the employee-owners voted to start using wind as their exclusive power source back in 1999—all the while knowing the decision would reduce their own end-of-year bonuses. Managers expected to see support for the move, since one of the 175-employee company's nine core values is "Environmental stewardship: minimizing resource consumption, maximizing energy efficiency, and recycling." Still, they couldn't help but be amazed when they called the question and every single hand went up. Pride in that vote has only increased in the eight years since, as employees have recognized how much CO_2 they've kept out of the atmosphere.

Building the cogeneration plant required another companywide leap of faith. New Belgium had been reclaiming steam and using it as a heat source since its basement-level brewing days, but it was going to cost $12 million to treat their wastewater, reclaim the methane generated, and use it to create electricity and heat at a scale necessary to fuel factory-level production. Once again, the 32-percent-employee-owned company bought in. But the payback on that investment shortened up in a hurry, thanks, in part, to several years of unprecedented hikes in energy prices. It also helped reduce the payback time that New Belgium didn't need expensive city water-treatment services anymore. At last word, New Belgium was saving an average of $8,000 a month by shaving their peak loads.

Why do Jeff and Kim devote so much effort to curtailing resource use and reducing their business's carbon footprint? Because "we want to," says Kim. She means, of course, that it fits their entrepreneurial ethos to do so. But, as we've seen, there are other reasons as well, most of them very hard-nosed business reasons. Jeff and Kim have discovered what we at Stonyfield Farm also know: that it truly pays—both in goodwill and at the bottom line—to be working continually and in every conceivable way to reduce emissions. The effort reduces the cost of operating the business while it builds brand loyalty among customers, and revenues come along for the ride. Doing the right thing also attracts corporate converts along the way. Several other specialty brewers have watched New Belgium succeed with CO_2 reduction measures and implemented similar strategies themselves. The first two, New York–based Brooklyn Brewery and Utah's Uinta Brewing Co., attributed their own decisions to switch to wind power to New Belgium's leadership.

I can just about guarantee that New Belgium will continue to lead in years to come—not in fast, flashy ways, but slowly, steadily, and without calling too much attention to itself as a company. Do remember that the image put forth by the brewery's best-known product is not Lance Armstrong's ultra-light speed machine, but a fat-tired cruising bike. This outfit is looking for incremental and sustainable gains, not quick sprints to the finish line. How do I know? Because New Belgium has taken the steps necessary to institutionalize its environmental commitment.

Like Stonyfield, New Belgium has put time and money into making plans that offer more than lip service, and it has challenged itself with lofty goals and tantalizing savings projections.

But most important, it has established clear lines of accountability for all of its CO_2-reducing strategies. And New Belgium has done it all by growing talent from within. The company recently created an executive-level sustainability director position and filled it with the former COO—a fourteen-year employee who was once the CFO as well.

The company and its environmental efforts have garnered plenty of awards, many of them at the national level. In 2004, New Belgium won the U.S. Environmental Protection Agency's prestigious Environmental Achievement Award for its multi-pronged approach to sustainability. New Belgium has also been recognized by the U.S. Department of Energy, the U.S. Green Building Council, and a variety of Colorado-based organizations. But one award, given in 2002, does perhaps the best job of describing what I think makes New Belgium Brewing so noteworthy. In an inscription on the Environmental Excellence Award given by *Business Ethics* magazine, the editors state: "Cofounders Kim Jordan, CEO, and her husband, Jeff Lebesch, are mindful of the need for sustainable growth rather than maximum growth. New Belgium Brewing is a place where quality of life—both for the environment and for humans—is central to their notion of business success."

Eileen Fisher's Mission: Making Green Fashionable

For many women, the line of clothing designed by Eileen Fisher is downright irresistible: simple, elegant, comfortable, understated, and made from natural linen, silk, and organic cotton fibers. My wife Meg, for one, is an addict, and she eagerly visits an Eileen Fisher Store every time we visit a city with an outlet. I like the way Meg looks in Eileen Fisher clothes—and I like the way they're sold, with an Earth-friendly message tailored to the line's socially conscious name-sake founder.

"What if we cared for our Earth's water as if every drop mattered?" That's the question posed on my computer screen alongside a picture of an attractive, middle-aged woman standing on the beach as a wave rolls ashore behind her.

Scroll down and click on a link "to learn how you can support our water supply." You'll find a page of laundry care instructions that emphasize saving energy and water and keeping harmful chemicals out of homes and waterways. There are also interesting facts about the Earth's water supply and how we use and abuse it, along with information about environmentally friendly Seventh Generation laundry products.

Welcome to the Eileen Fisher, Inc., Web site, the online presence of a wholly uncommon kind of women's clothing design and manufacturing company based not in the garment district of New York City, but in the bucolic village of Irvington, New York. From its outpost in one of the historic Hudson River towns just north of Manhattan, the company and its founder supply upscale department stores and trendy boutiques with a comfortable, understated line of women's clothing.

Green may not be the uniform shade of the Eileen Fisher–designed jackets, pants, skirts, and tops gracing retail displays, but her notion of sustaining health and wellness—for employees, customers, and, by extension, the planet we all share—has long been the driving philosophy underlying the company's business. The latest evolutionary wrinkle is the formal acknowledgment of environmental concerns in the company's mission statement. Now Eileen Fisher's stated purpose of inspiring "simplicity, creativity, and delight through connection and great design" is extended in practice to include environmental sustainability as one of its social-consciousness initiatives, right alongside support for the well-being of women and an absolute commitment to human rights.

Today, the Eileen Fisher company is concentrating on getting sustainable fabrics into its product line, reducing paper and plastic waste at the retail level, and incorporating recycled materials in the design and construction of its stores and offices. Its first Eco Audit, which is currently under way, will help gauge the environmental impact of its operations, set realistic sustainability goals, and identify ways to achieve them.

For customers, the most visible incarnation of the company's environmental focus is its introduction of a line of clothing using organic cotton fibers. The new items have been enthusiastically received, according to Amy Hall, the company's director of social consciousness. Sales of hand-knit organic cotton sweaters from Peru and other organic pieces in the designer's 2007 spring collection accounted for nearly 9 percent of overall sales in March, more than doubling the year-earlier share, Hall says. The growing interest in organic fibers is a trend that is expected to accelerate.

For Eileen Fisher and the company that bears her name, a commitment to using eco fibers is about more than just producing good-looking clothing with a luxurious feel. The passionate commitment extends to the health and well-being of the farmers who grow the cotton, the workers who weave the fabrics and manufacture the garments, and those Fisher employees who shepherd the clothes from warehouse to selling floor and into the customers' hands.

The company's manufacturing facilities in China, Uruguay, Peru, India, and New York must meet tough and comprehensive workplace standards based on United Nations and International Labor Organization conventions. Generally known as Social Accountability 8000, or SA8000, the standards address child labor, forced labor, freedom of association, disciplinary practices, discrimination, working hours, remuneration, health, safety, and management systems. Furthermore, the Fisher company partners with two social compliance audit organizations to make sure its workplace demands are being met. It has been lauded as one of only three U.S.-based companies to enforce these tough requirements on a global scale. For Chinese workers, in particular, making Fisher clothing may be their first exposure to a safe and healthy work environment, reinforcing the company's belief that holding fast to its principles "can help facilitate change from within."

Although the privately held company doesn't disclose profit numbers, in 2006 it rang up sales of $225 million, a figure that indicates an 83 percent overall increase in sales since 2002. Four-year sales growth of that magnitude is not bad in any industry, but it's especially noteworthy in the notoriously dicey women's clothing business.

With her combination of fashion sense, business acumen, and social conscience, Fisher has built a company profitable enough to provide its roughly 776 wholesale and retail employees with benefits seldom seen in the clothing trade—traditional health insurance, for instance. It also gives each employee a $1,000 education stipend each year, along with a $1,000 wellness benefit to be used on restorative measures like massages, holistic spa treatments, and nutritional counseling. The company also hosts free on-site yoga, tai chi, and dance classes as well as meditation sessions to relieve stress. Not much stress would seem to be job-related, though, since the company discourages its employees from working long hours and actively encourages them to maintain a healthy balance between work and the lives they lead outside the office.

If this company and its mission seem to bear little if any resemblance to the intense, sometimes nasty atmosphere commonly associated with New York's Seventh Avenue fashion industry, credit the style and vision of the real-life woman whose hand is on the tiller. Eileen Fisher's personal mission has always been to encourage individual growth and well-being among the people around her.

Starting in 1984 with $350, a degree in home economics, and a distaste for clothes that never seemed to fit her properly, Eileen's desire to make women feel good about themselves and their bodies has provided the inspiration for her clothing designs and her charitable causes. Through the company's grant-making program and in-store events, more than $890,000 in cash and products was distributed to nearly one hundred nonprofit organizations in 2006, many of them with missions focused on women and families. The company also provides direct aid to women entrepreneurs who have a great idea and a strong business plan to back it up through their annual Business Grant Program for Woman Entrepreneurs. And to encourage employees' charitable impulses, Eileen

Fisher matches contributions up to $1,000 per employee each year.

For an entrepreneur like Eileen Fisher, who values sustainability in the workplace and the world and considers monetary rewards a secondary benefit, what are the gratifying paybacks? For one thing, a growing list of satisfied customers who make it possible for Eileen to finance the extraordinary perks she gives her employees and the comfortable yet simple life she has forged for herself and her family. For another, a skinny employee turnover rate that ends up saving her company upward of $325,000 a year in recruiting and retraining costs. Then there are the studies that show a correlation between wellness programs and health-care costs; for every dollar spent, the return over a one- to six-year period ranges between $3.40 and $6.15.

But most of all, Eileen Fisher has the satisfaction of knowing that she is making people feel good about themselves and making our planet a better place to live.

"You know, if you're paying attention to what you care about and what you love—and for me, how the whole thing comes together," Fisher told a CBS News correspondent not long ago, "then it tends to work at the bottom line." After all, as she pointed out, the bottom line is nothing more than "numbers that reflect what's happening in the center." It follows that if you do what's right at the center, the bottom line will take care of itself. And it has.

For Stonyfield, as for other sustainable businesses, the secret of success is staying true to yourself and never betraying your mission. At the heart of every thriving business is a unique selling proposition. Sustainable companies are no different, but the standards we set for ourselves are higher, harder, riskier—and more rewarding. That's what our customers expect. What could be more fun than exceeding those expectations?

In the next chapter, I'll tell how I surprised even myself in cutting Stonyfield's carbon emissions, and go on to show powerful examples of other companies, big and small, doing the same.

3

From CO_2 Toward CO_{NO}

In 2003, knowing that it was more symbolic than practical, we installed New Hampshire's largest solar electric array on the roof of our Yogurt Works in Londonderry. Skeptics sneered. At a cost of hundreds of thousands of dollars, I wanted to extract solar energy from skies that aren't exactly in the Sun Belt. Moreover, oil was then relatively cheap; a gallon of gasoline cost about $1.60. The numbers indicated a long wait for any payback—at least twelve years, if ever.

My sister, Nancy, our vice president of natural resources, Lisa Drake, our natural resources manager, and I persisted: Someone had to prove that replacing fossil fuels made good business sense. We believed that renewable sources of energy were essential in the battle against carbon pollution and global warming. And while the near-term economics were not favorable, we knew that Stonyfield could not stand by and just preach this philosophy. We needed to demonstrate our commitment. Even a modest payback would be cause for celebration, I thought.

Little did I know that oil prices were about to soar, even before our first fifty-thousand-watt array was up and running. Suddenly our payback schedule was cut by almost half, and our experiment proved that solar power can boost the bottom line. Recent technology improvements would result in an even faster payback.

Speaking of profits, a business has only two ways to make them—you can either increase revenue or cut costs. It is patently clear that nothing is more costly, both monetarily and environmentally, than sticking with carbon-spewing, planet-warming fossil fuels. Whether you're using time, money, labor, or energy, a businessperson has to keep plugging leaks. The results can be pleasantly surprising.

Carbon-cutting has saved Stonyfield literally millions of dollars—a revenue stream that I call the First National Bank of Conservation. However, for our first decade, as we fought and kicked our way to reach the break-even point, we didn't quite grasp that our cost-cutting efforts had a larger purpose than taming the bottom line. They turned out to be field exercises in subverting the traditional business mind-set, which views costs only in dollar terms.

As I mentioned in Chapter 1, nature is the most efficient and cost-effective system in the universe. Heeding its organizing and operating principles will, in my view, put any business on course to sustainable (in every sense) wealth. But no such cosmic thought hit me for many years. Only in 1980, while helping to build windmills in New Mexico, did I begin to see the real light.

Ranchers there and across the West put up windmills to tap aquifers and maintain water for cattle in thousands of tanks sited on vast stretches of rangeland. Electric pumps are too expensive and impractical. Beyond that, wind-driven water pumps have proved their reliability, which counts for a lot when a power failure could result in cattle dying of thirst. Even if ranchers could afford them, remote power lines are vulnerable. Windmills avoid that risk and have the added virtue of not belching carbon into the atmosphere.

For generations, those ranchers have put their trust in tried-and-true solutions dependent on sustainable processes. Their lore and their success made a deep impression on me as well. My realization that nature is a reliable source of knowledge and wisdom informed a lot of what we eventually tried to accomplish at Stonyfield.

Like other evangelists, of course, I did not immediately dazzle multitudes of converts. I had to accept that one person's gospel may be another's yawn. In China, when I preached sustainability to scientists and students in the early 1980s, I got back only blank smiles. When I tried to excite Chinese farmers about the natural beauties of wind and solar power and organic farming, they reacted as if I had served them week-old dumplings. Yoked to ancient, back-breaking practices, they yearned for the symbols of high-tech capitalism. The watch on my wrist triggered a far bigger buzz than all my talk about sustainability.

Eventually, it dawned on me that sermonizing would never get my ecological ideas into mainstream thinking. I had to marry those ideas to a business proposition. Unless I could show that real money lurked in curbing carbon, my cause would never attract enough believers to fill a phone booth, let alone save the planet.

I focus on energy because the way humans use it can propel our species toward either suicide or salvation. I use business as my platform because it's the world's prime energy consumer. In this era of global warming, every polluting company is a microcosm of humankind's choices. Those that find ways to shrink their carbon footprint can become rich survivors. Those that stay dirty are literally headed for the dustbin of history.

In business, you can manage energy use to great effect. You can determine exactly what you're spending on energy for every product made or sold. And that's what we did. We installed good insulation and switched to energy-saving lightbulbs. We replaced old, wasteful oil burners with new boilers that use natural gas and have sophisticated controls. Our local utility, which offers efficiency credits, gave us a rebate for building a refrigerated cold-storage building with extra-thick walls that keep cool air in and warm air out.

From 1995 to 2005 we increased our efficiency, saving more than 46 million kilowatt hours. That's enough to power 4,500 homes for a year and prevent some 14,000 tons of carbon dioxide from entering the atmosphere. The savings go directly to our bottom line: We're $1.6 million wealthier on this item alone.

Capitalizing on what we've learned over the past twenty years, Stonyfield looks at curbing carbon as a moneymaking means to a larger end—identifying profitable alternatives to conventional ways of doing business, ways that allow us and other companies to operate in sustainable ways. We think reducing energy use is an excellent route forward.

It can also be an eye-opening process. I have learned, for example, that some of my assumptions about energy use may well turn out to be false. Early on, I discovered that selling locally doesn't necessarily save fuel costs, which may, in fact, be cheaper when you sell farther away.

I stumbled on that paradox in 1986, when I set out to compare the per-unit energy cost of delivering one package of yogurt to retailers in New York City and another in nearby Burlington, Vermont. The result surprised me: Even though the trip to Burlington took only two hours versus five hours to New York, the Burlington package used three times as much energy, which, of course, dramatically increased our costs. Because the trucks bound for New York carried full loads while the trucks to Burlington were only partly loaded, the energy used by each New York truck was spread over more yogurt cups. I couldn't believe it. Later, when we were sending whole truckloads to New York, we did even better: We found a poultry producer who was driving up to New England from Maryland with a full load of chickens and driving back empty. We contracted to provide his return loads, got a great low rate, and concluded that since he would be driving the return route anyway, the delivery increased pollution only by the small amount of extra fuel needed to haul the load. We've been doing business with him for over a decade.

But that was still an unsophisticated view of the real environmental issue. To measure Stonyfield's true impact on the planet, we had to measure our carbon footprint. I asked Nancy to take on this enormously complicated task.

Plug by Plug: Nancy Takes Us Carbon-Neutral

It's estimated that every American generates twenty-three tons of carbon dioxide each year—by driving, cooking, heating and cooling our homes, flicking the switch on electrical appliances, and consuming food that was produced by someone else burning oil and natural gas. While reducing our individual use of energy is essential, no matter how many days you leave your car at home and walk or take the bus to work, or how many cans and bottles you recycle, or how many lights you switch off, you still won't completely erase your carbon footprint. What's more, the carbon emitted by businesses dwarfs that of individuals many times over. Stonyfield, it turned out to my chagrin, was no exception.

In 1992, as ecological and economical calculations improved, Nancy joined the company. She began asking questions: Where do we want to go regarding carbon reduction, and how do we plan to get there? How will we measure our progress?

Around 1994, Nancy started working with our managers to identify Stonyfield's environmental impacts and the appropriate indicators we would use to gauge our successes. The first step was to pinpoint how we affected the environment. She identified four main areas of concern—greenhouse gas emissions, toxins, resource use, and waste generated by our operations—and she then began reporting on them monthly. It was a start.

We created a "Mission Report," which outlined the way we affected the environment—from water used in our factory to the toxic load from the growing of the ingredients we used to make our yogurt. We began an ambitious waste minimization program and packaging reduction initiatives and launched our organic products—which greatly reduced our toxic load on the planet.

While all of the ways we affect the environment are significant, the biggest issue facing our generation—and several more to come—is climate change. Over the past decade, our understanding of how Stonyfield's operations contribute to global warming has evolved. Back in 1996 it was very clear to us that one of our key contributions to global warming was the energy we used in our plant to make yogurt. While we were focused on efforts to increase efficiency and decrease emissions, at the end of the day, we were still using energy and putting global warming gases into the atmosphere. We had heard of an electric utility that had begun "offsetting" the CO_2 emissions from its energy use by investing in reforestation projects whereby trees would absorb an amount of CO_2 equivalent to what their power plants were generating.

Since the concept was relatively new, information was not widely available. After months of work, and with the guidance of Dr. Mark Trexler, who had recently left the World Resources Institute (WRI) to help companies with climate mitigation strategies, Stonyfield began a program to offset 100 percent of the emissions from our facility energy use through investments in projects that would absorb CO_2 (like tree planting), or prevent it from being released (like wind power, which displaces conventional power), becoming the first U.S. manufacturer to become carbon-neutral. Since the process had been so arduous, we published a booklet, *The Carbon Cookbook,* which we made available for free to other businesses on how they could do it, too.

As we continued to reduce our carbon footprint, we realized that we needed to dig deeper. We knew the impact of our growing factory's energy use, and we assumed it was one of our greatest (or rather worst) contributions to global warming. We were in for a surprise.

In 1999, working with Tim Greiner of Pure Strategies, we completed a detailed and ambitious appraisal of our entire carbon footprint—a tally of all the energy we use and all the carbon our operations shoot into the atmosphere. The analysis entailed a complex reckoning: We had to add up the energy we burned and take ownership of everything, from the global-warming-causing methane our garbage generated in the city landfill to the gargantuan amounts of methane that were being burped, farted, and pooped by our cows. We looked at the energy used by our trucks shipping yogurt and bringing ingredients to our factory, as well as the materials themselves.

We have repeated this detailed carbon footprinting since 2000 and the two biggest culprits have remained the same: the cows, including both their methane emissions and greenhouse gas emissions from growing and transporting feed for them, and our packaging. Shipping the yogurt is our third-biggest carbon producer. Fourth is the energy used to run our plant.

Drawing up a carbon footprint is a valuable tool for any business to understand its contribution to global warming, and to help identify priorities in mitigating the impact. At Stonyfield, we know where our impacts are, have set goals in each of the areas, and have teams working on shrinking our carbon footprint—beyond the walls of our yogurt works—deep into our supply chain, through to the trucking of our products to the store.

Of course, there's always room for improvement, and we will never finish our cleanup. Thanks to Nancy and her team's unstinting efforts, though, we now have a more sophisticated reading of the exact trouble spots and the people responsible for them.

In 2006, we created the Mission Action Plan (MAP). A team of managers has identified ten different problem areas and set concrete goals for fixing them, thus making it impossible for anyone to shirk responsibility. For instance, the packaging people are charged with reducing energy use by a set amount, and will be held accountable in performance reviews. Our aim has been to get all employees, not just the managers, emotionally connected to our long-term environmental goals.

Meanwhile, teams of Stonyfield colleagues are considering ways to lessen the carbon produced by methane emissions from the cows and our packaging. Dietary changes are the obvious solution to the former problem, but what mix of grains, how much to feed, and at which times of day are all questions that must be researched before definitive answers can be given.

Companies, and individuals, too, can calculate their carbon footprint, of course, and now, a decade or more since we wrote *The Carbon Cookbook*, there is an abundance of resources on the Internet to help. As Nancy says, it's not about perfection. It's really all about identifying where your impact is and what the priorities are and taking steps to mitigate the impact. The key is to look at the big picture with one simple message in mind: "From CO_2 toward CO_{NO}."

That's the rule we strive to follow at Stonyfield. But given the impossibility of manufacturing anything without expending energy, and the challenges of incorporating renewables into our energy supply, we know that it will be a long time before we'll ever be able to eliminate all of our carbon emissions. However, we can reduce most of them, and then we can offset what remains by supporting projects that prevent or reduce emissions elsewhere.

We have continued to offset 100 percent of the CO_2 from our facility energy use every year since 1997. I know offsets are controversial because, without being coupled to a program of emissions reductions, they are the equivalent of what a U.K. friend has called a "morning-after pill." Properly administered, though, offsets can be very effective. Offsets will certainly be part of a successful national energy policy, as will a cap-and-trade system. Under such a system, polluting companies purchase other organizations' emission credits as a sort of Earth tax or penalty to offset the inevitable emissions of greenhouse gases.

At Stonyfield, these offset projects link us to a whole network of outside organizations that are pooling diverse abilities to save and strengthen the balance of nature on this planet. Among our offset investments have been the Oregon Forest Resource Trust, which replants deforested watersheds and riparian habitats in Oregon, thus improving wildlife habitat, water quality, soil stability, and the recovery of endangered salmon. In northern China, we funded a project to build straw-bale houses, which reduced local coal burning as much as 90 percent—a boon to human health and longevity.

In Ohio and other states, we financed methane-recovery projects that capture and use gas vented from sealed coal mines. Methane gas—a more powerful contributor to global warming, some say, than carbon dioxide—builds up inside coal mines and must be constantly vented to prevent explosions, often for twenty or thirty years after a mine stops operating. Until now, this gas was simply released into the open air. With methane recovery, the vented gas is diverted to generators to produce electricity, instead of being allowed to pollute the atmosphere.

In a similar venture, we collaborated with NativeEnergy in Vermont to help a wastewater-treatment plant use its methane by-product to run electricity-generating turbines for New England. Near St. Francis, South Dakota, again allied with NativeEnergy, we helped the Rosebud Sioux Indian Tribe develop a wind turbine that generates clean power, sharply decreasing carbon emissions in the area.

We are working on some longer-term projects to further reduce our carbon footprint—for instance, to extend credit to employees who switch to hybrid vehicles for commuting to work, or set up our own fleet of hybrid or natural gas–powered vans to carry employees to and from work.

The imperative for every business and individual to leave a smaller carbon footprint is profound. Adopting energy-efficient technologies, incorporating renewables, and redesigning our manufacturing processes to use less energy are essential to prevent enormous climate change and disruption to our economy—and in most cases, they are good for business profitability too. Offsets are not a panacea—and will not reverse global warming—but they can do some good in the world.

Effectively paying employees to join the CEO's crusade may irk some purists. I don't disagree. I would hate to see any company's carbon correctness slide into political correctness, real or imagined. Fortunately, there's a new business in the United States that may take corporate paternalism out of the picture. I refer to the sellers of America's fastest-growing energy alternative, so-called green tags. The tags give ordinary people an easy way to support clean energy sources like wind and solar power by paying a fee to offset their own carbon emissions.

Take TerraPass, for example. This for-profit company in

Menlo Park, California, sells green tags costing as much as $80 a year to drivers looking for a way to balance out the CO_2 their cars disgorge into the atmosphere. The company's revenues come from a portion of the fees that it charges drivers, with most of the money going to support nine renewable energy projects, from wind farms to producers of biofuels. TerraPass has more than 2,400 members, and it says their purchases of green tags have offset the emission of 36 million pounds of carbon—the annual equivalent of taking six thousand cars off the road. For the vast number of Americans who may be worried about global warming but dependent on their cars for transportation, green tags from TerraPass allow them to do something about the problem without having to give up their livelihoods and lifestyles.

But it's not just drivers who are reaching for the green passes. Skiers buy $2 tags along with their lift tickets to offset the energy they must use to get to the slopes, and eco-friendly friends of couples about to be wed in faraway places purchase the tags to assuage their consciences and offset the fuel their jet burns in getting them to the wedding site. One such green-tagger muses that getting any new technology off the ground takes incentives, and this one seems to fit the bill for many friends of the Earth.

Many more of America's biggest and best-known companies, including IBM, Starbucks, Liz Claiborne, and Johnson & Johnson, meet their renewable energy targets and reduce overall carbon emissions by buying offsets from 3 Phases Energy Services. This San Francisco middleman earns a half cent on every kilowatt hour that is offset and passes the rest of the funds to forty wind farms around the country.

The wind farms are then able to lower the price of the usually uncompetitive power they generate and sell it to local customers, thereby reducing those users' dependence on polluting power sources. Starbucks, IBM, and the rest continue to burn power generated by fossil fuels, while also helping to develop alternative energy sources that may one day be able to provide enough power to service all those companies and individuals who would use them if they were more affordable and available in their areas.

Any business, no matter how small, can get into the game. Inspiration can be found in green businesses like Harbec Plastics in Ontario, New York, a $12-million-a-year enterprise that puts much larger companies to shame with its amazingly efficient, injection-molded plastic-parts manufacturing operation. Owner Bob Bechtold, a tireless environmentalist, generates nearly all of the 1 million kilowatt hours of electricity he needs each year from on-site installations. Some 75 percent of the energy comes from a natural-gas-fueled microturbine power plant, with another 20 percent generated by a 130-foot-tall wind turbine. As for the other 5 percent of power the factory needs, he reduces that with skylights. Bechtold also uses the heat thrown off by his power plant in a cogeneration process that runs heating and air-conditioning equipment, saving around $20,000 a month. "Haunted," he says, "by the thought that the environment is not mine to waste," he has created an enviable record.

But a small company has limits. Bigger businesses can do much more. Adobe Systems, for one, turned itself into the greenest corporate site in America and won highest honors from the U.S. Green Building Council in 2006. The $2 billion software maker earned its accolades by instituting a list of energy-saving measures at its headquarters in San Jose, California, that slashed electricity use by 35 percent and gas use by 41 percent in just five years, even as its employee rolls jumped by 80 percent. The company spent $1.1 million on motion-sensing light switches, waterless urinals, automatic faucets, and fluorescent lights, among other things, which paid for themselves in just over a year and now continue to add millions to Adobe's bottom line.

But what if all the companies in the *Fortune* 500 became carbon-neutral? Think of giants like General Electric, General Motors, and General Mills. Imagine the impact:

- If only fifty-three large companies went carbon-neutral, the United States would meet the proposed Kyoto Protocol target of reducing 1.5 billion metric tons of CO_2 equivalent from current net emissions.
- If every *Fortune* 500 company cut greenhouse gas emissions by just 5 percent, the United States could meet almost half of the Kyoto target.
- If half of the *Fortune* 500 companies reduced their emissions by 5 percent, they would stop spewing as much carbon every year as can be absorbed by 94 million acres of trees.
- If just one hundred large companies lowered their emissions by 5 percent, it would be equivalent to taking 25 million cars off the road for a year.

Now imagine what would happen if the vast U.S. government—with its myriad branches, buildings, offices, machines, and military equipment—were to get serious about cutting emissions.

In Europe, companies are required to obey specific emission limits, with some flexibility allowed. Businesses that beat their quotas can sell their unused emissions in the form of credits to other corporations that are exceeding their own quotas. In a continent-wide trading system, the buyers currently pay about $40 per metric ton of carbon discharged into the atmosphere.

Some people oppose this system, arguing that it's wrong to license pollution. But I think it's a good idea. It turns carbon pollution into a cost of doing business, and makes carbon reduction a source of revenue. The system converts green behavior from an ideological frill to good business—which means it will spread rapidly.

And some companies are going considerably further than present laws require. Consider giant General Electric, whose Ecomagination program sets a new standard in green commitment for American industry. GE has made four major pledges:

- To spend $1.5 billion a year on research in cleaner technologies by 2010, doubling the pace of 2005.
- To raise revenues to at least $20 billion by 2010 from such products as wind-power generators, diesel-electric hybrid locomotives, "cleaner coal" technologies, and advanced water treatment systems.
- To reduce its greenhouse gas emissions by 30 percent and raise energy efficiency by 30 percent by 2012.
- To report on its progress in meeting all these goals, publicly and transparently, whether or not it succeeds.

It's fair to say that if all the *Fortune* 500 companies were to match GE's commitment, we'd be well along the road to bringing global warming under control.

To help other companies find their footing in this process, Stonyfield has mobilized a group of activists, including the nonprofit group Clean Air–Cool Planet, to devise a progress checker, the Climate Counts Scorecard. I serve as chairman of Climate Counts. We annually audit business' practices and give them a baseline that they can use to improve their ratings from year to year. Available at Stonyfield.com and at climatecounts.org, the scorecard has four sections (*Review*, *Reduce*, *Report,* and *Policy*) that measure a company's carbon footprint by asking a series of questions and scoring the answers on a hundred-point scale.

Review poses six questions to determine the thoroughness of a company's emissions inventory on a scale of 0 to 20. *Reduce* asks twelve questions that assess a company's carbon-cutting program, with a top score of 68. *Report* presents two queries that provide a reading on the company's actual progress toward a healthy climate. Finally, *Policy* has two questions that assess the company's support of climate legislation.

The point system is aimed at fair, neutral analysis of an organization's environmental impact. Devoid of praise or criticism, it simply shows companies how they can improve their efforts over time. But the analysis is also put on public record, accessible to anyone. Just participating shows a corporation's willingness to be embarrassed by slow progress. Conversely, the system provides annual benchmarks allowing a company to prove that its environmental commitment is serious, not just PR puffery.

With numerous companies already assessed, the Climate Counts rating system's public access may well create a sort of jury, including consumers, investors, media, competitors, suppliers, and anyone else with an interest in a business's carbon-cutting progress. Investors can use a company's rating in their share-buying decisions. Consumers can vote with their dollars. Companies themselves may choose to advertise a score higher than a competitor's.

Full disclosure: In our first annual audit, Stonyfield itself registered only in the 60s on our Climate Counts Scorecard, partly because our offsets don't count nearly as heavily toward improving the climate as do absolute reductions in carbon emissions, like implementing more renewable energy systems. But we scored far better than most companies and, more important, we now have an additional objective road map for how to prioritize our next investment.

In my view, any pressure on the brakes as the planet speeds toward disaster can only be considered positive progress. These efforts also engender tremendous consumer and employee pride and loyalty. An excellent example of a company that is applying the brakes while also steering in a totally new direction is Timberland, which, like Stonyfield, calls New Hampshire home.

A Label for a Healthy Environment

I admit to a special fondness for Timberland and Jeff Swartz, grandson of the founder and now its chief executive. That's in part because of our shared heritage in the shoe trade—my father and grandfather owned shoe factories in Pittsfield, Newmarket, and Laconia, New Hampshire. But what I most admire about this $1.6 billion company is this: Under Jeff's guidance, the corporation has become a passionate steward of the environment and a role model for others. Ardent about the need to protect and preserve natural habitats while also minimizing the company's carbon footprint, Jeff and the people he leads truly share my belief that business is the answer to the planet's predicament.

Jeff is a high-spirited Bostonian who blazes with moneymaking ideas, jokes, and a zest for life lived in what he calls the "nexus of commerce and justice," a space in which business can operate in harmony with humankind's economic, social, and ecological interests and still make a handsome profit.

Timberland is publicly traded yet family-controlled, allowing Jeff to stress that profits and the environment are equally important to him: "I believe that the idea we're trying to sell—sustainability—depends not on either/or, but on both." It's only a matter of time, he insists, before consumers demand that companies show a commitment to the environment. Even Timberland's slogan—"Boot, Brand, Belief"—reflects Jeff's notion that succeeding in business is not an end in itself, but rather a means to help spread the gospel of environmental sanity.

Having already made significant cuts in Timberland's greenhouse-gas emissions, Jeff has set his sights on making the company's U.S. operations carbon-neutral by 2010. Right now, he's converting Timberland's offices to electricity generated by renewable sources. An array of solar cells already stands outside the company's Stratham headquarters.

At the company's California distribution center, 1,932 more solar panels supply 60 percent of the center's energy, forestalling the emission of 480,000 pounds of carbon each year. The company's Dominican Republic manufacturing plant generates power with a blend of solar panels and wind generators. Its distribution center in Holland runs on a triple play of wind, waste-steam, and hydro power. Timberland is revamping its truck fleet to save fuel and stem carbon emissions. To offset its remaining emissions, it's buying T-RECs (tradable renewable energy credits, a form of green tags) that help fund renewable power sources.

Although Timberland is voluntarily buying the T-RECs, Jeff is not a big fan of carbon offsets. He shares my U.K. friend's morning-after pill analogy, but likens them to acquiring a papal dispensation to disobey some ecclesiastical law. So he is primarily working to eliminate Timberland's emissions altogether. I agree with Jeff that zero emissions should be our ultimate goal, but we won't get there anytime soon—not until we make bigger and better strides in the generation, storage, and use of renewable energy. In the meantime, those of us in the goods-producing sector will have to rely at least partially on some form of fossil fuel.

As in all businesses, Timberland's goals as a company depend on the efforts of its employees, and it encourages them through a variety of programs. Timberland offers $3,000 to every employee who buys a hybrid car. It makes the deal even more attractive by setting aside prime parking spots at its headquarters for those who carpool or wheel a hybrid into the lot.

Nothing is overlooked in Jeff's campaign to make Timberland a leader in the drive to heal our ailing planet. Even its product packaging and labeling are now eco-friendly, or "nutritional," as the company likes to say. "Nutritional" labeling is an ingeniously simple idea—one adapted from the food industry but a first for apparel retailing—that aims to make customers champions of the environment through smarter buying.

The labeling educates consumers as to the manufacturing, environmental, and community impacts of a Timberland product based on where the product was made; how much total energy went into producing it, and how much of that was generated by renewable sources. It also assesses how Timberland affects the communities in which it operates as measured against its Code of Conduct, which forbids child labor and sets standards for hours worked, freedom of association, compensation, workplace conditions, and health and safety.

Convinced that customers will soon demand just the kind of information he is providing, Jeff envisions a shoe shopper at, say, Nordstrom, asking to try on boots. The Nordstrom sales associate returns with two possibilities, both well made, both attractive. Sliding a foot into first one brand and then the other, the customer notices that the Timberland boot has a label outlining its environmental and community impact, but the other brand doesn't.

"Why doesn't this more expensive boot have this kind of label?" the customer asks the associate. The associate doesn't have an answer. No matter; the customer is already settling on the Timberland boot. It looks and feels great, it costs less, and, better yet, its manufacturer is concerned about the same environmental issues that worry the customer.

For Jeff, though, the label isn't so much about beating a rival as it is about shaming his competitors into adopting the Timberland level of commitment and transparency. He believes the marketplace will force opaque companies to adopt the kind of eco-friendly measures that Timberland supports, and all of us will be better for it.

To complement its nutritional labels, Timberland is introducing footwear boxes made of 100 percent post-consumer, recycled-waste fiber. The boxes also use water-based solvents in place of chemical glues, and the labels are printed with soy-based, rather than traditional petroleum-based, inks.

Consumers find their own call to action when they open a new Timberland box. The boxes include:

- A message asking: "What kind of footprint will you leave?"—a prompt for customers to get involved in environmental activities.
- Tissue wrapping for children's footwear that is printed with interesting, educational information about birds and other animals.

Yet another evolution in Timberland packaging and labeling appeared in the spring of 2007, when the company introduced its Green Index hang tag on five outdoor products. Consumers can now gauge on a scale of zero to ten how the product rates in terms of greenhouse-gas emissions, chemicals and solvents used in its manufacture, and the quantity of organic, renewable, and recycled materials the product contains.

What it all comes down to, Jeff explains, is "letting the customer lead himself" to environmentally friendly products. He believes this is really the only option a business has. And at Timberland, where the chief executive is intimately involved with the product and is making critical cost and carbon decisions at various points along the way, the label is one of the few tools he has to educate the consumer about his company's practices in a matter-of-fact, "thought-you-might-want-to-know" kind of way.

Critics may dismiss the Timberland scion as a self-appointed savior preaching from a shoe box, but believers like me laud Jeff as a welcome voice for a new age of environmental awareness. For his part, Jeff, who is keenly attuned to the condition of his profit-and-loss statement, is particularly irked by those who claim that his business is likely to suffer from his focus on the environment instead of investors' desire for ever greater profits. "What idiot will leave costs on the table?" he rhetorically asked a member of the press, referring to the cost savings produced by being energy-efficient. "I hope it's our competitors. I get paid to create value."

That's exactly what he's doing. Through the end of 2006, Timberland's annual sales and earnings have kept growing. Record revenue and net income were accompanied by strong cash generation and greater returns for shareholders.

And the hard numbers of Timberland's success were buttressed by a string of accolades. *Fortune* and *Forbes* both listed Timberland in their "best companies to work for" lists. Winslow Management gave the company its Green2 award for benefiting the environment as well as shareholders, while Clean Air–Cool Planet chose Timberland as its "Climate Champion." Other awards honored Timberland as one of the best corporate citizens, best-managed manufacturers, and best companies for working mothers.

Jeff is determined to leave a bootprint on the business terrain, and he's clearly made a good start. Besides its commitment to the environment, the company he leads provides in-house day care for employees' children and forty hours of paid time off each year for community service. Timberland also supports City Year, a sort of urban Peace Corps that the company helped found to recruit a diverse group of young people for twelve-month internships as public employees in Boston and other cities. Then there's Serv-a-palooza, Timberland's annual day-long outburst of civic service that, in 2005, hosted 170 projects in 27 countries, amassing 45,000 volunteer hours of charitable work.

Jeff Swartz's inspired portfolio of ideas for making his business a force for the environment has made him a cultural role model for companies of all sizes, including mine. I am particularly interested in adapting his nutritional label to track Stonyfield's progress toward our own goal of carbon neutrality. In fact, every manufacturer's products ought to carry such a label. As Jeff likes to say, "What you do is who you are."

Wal-Mart's Carbon Consciousness

Wal-Mart is the world's biggest company, and because it has $315 billion in annual sales and sixty thousand suppliers in a vast range of industries, any change in its methods and practices reverberates on businesses around the world. So it's good news indeed that under CEO Lee Scott, Wal-Mart is now focusing on sustainability.

Wal-Mart's impact on the environment is staggering. But according to *Fortune* magazine, it is now seeking to cut its carbon emissions by 25 percent and double the fuel efficiency of its mammoth, 6,900-truck fleet (which currently consumes an estimated 134,158,000 gallons of diesel fuel each year). It also aims to reduce energy use in its more than 6,600 big-box stores by 20 to 30 percent and convert to 100 percent renewable energy sources. To hint at what those moves might mean, Wal-Mart's 2,074 U.S. supercenters alone use a total of 3.11 billion kilowatts of electricity per year—that's the same amount of electricity used by the city of San Francisco.

Lee Scott was first drawn to sustainability because efficient use of resources makes such good dollar-and-cent sense. Just one of his reforms, doubling the trucking fleet's efficiency, might save the company $300 million per year. Who wouldn't grab that kind of savings with both hands? How much more product would Wal-Mart need to sell to add that much to the bottom line?

Scott is investing $500 million in sustainability projects and has already opened two superstores that incorporate advanced climate-control and water-conservation systems, along with renewable power sources such as solar and wind power and recyclable building materials like bamboo. Five years ago, who could have imagined a Wal-Mart store heated by a biofuel boiler that burns used cooking oil from the in-store café and motor oil salvaged from its auto-service center? If this isn't a sign of creeping environmental sanity, I don't know what is.

To get a better sense of what's going on at Wal-Mart, I took a tour of its Web site, including an interactive feature called "The Road to Sustainability: Starting the Journey." I quickly learned that Wal-Mart has formed a partnership with the National Wildlife Federation to conserve one acre of wildlife habitat for every acre of Wal-Mart development; it has also promised to contribute $35 million over ten years to protect important fish, wildlife, and plant resources.

The company is also investing in lighter, more aerodynamic trucks with fuel-efficient engines and tires, hybrid drive systems, and auxiliary power units that heat or cool a truck when the driver stops for a break, thus allowing the main engine to be shut down. This change alone, the company says, will reduce carbon output by 100,000 metric tons a year and, with diesel fuel selling in the neighborhood of $3 a gallon, will save nearly $30 million in annual fuel costs.

In its stores, Wal-Mart is installing doors on previously open refrigerated cases, cutting the cooling load by 70 percent, and replacing fluorescent lighting in the cases with long-lasting LED (light-emitting diode) lighting, which slices the energy load in half and practically eliminates maintenance costs. Old-fashioned incandescent bulbs in its ceiling fans are being replaced with compact fluorescent lightbulbs, a seemingly small change that will save $7 million a year in electricity and prevent utilities from burning an estimated five hundred pounds of coal over the lifetime of each bulb to generate it.

Remarkably, Wal-Mart has also confronted the "big box" syndrome—those oversized, energy-wasting packages that shout a brand name and hog shelf space. Suppliers often assume bigger is better. Wal-Mart has a clever new way to prove the opposite. If a soap manufacturer, say, agrees to downsize a detergent—concentrating the same amount in a smaller package—Wal-Mart will designate it as a volume-producing item (VPI). VPIs are displayed prominently on store shelves and heavily promoted to customers. Scott instructs salespeople to stress that downsized packaging is an energy-saving value all around. The smaller a container, the less energy it takes at every stage, from production to shipping to disposal.

Wal-Mart's new green philosophy extends beyond energy efficiency. When Scott learned that 190,000 units of a yoga outfit made out of organic cotton disappeared from Sam's Club shelves in just ten weeks, he became interested in organic products, too. Now Wal-Mart has made multiyear commitments for 8 to 10 million metric tons a year of pesticide-free cotton. That's 1.5 to 3.5 million more tons than growers could reasonably have hoped to sell to all their buyers put together before Wal-Mart charged into the market. Wal-Mart is also the world's top seller of organic milk and a purveyor of many other organic foods.

It's easy to imagine the late Sam Walton himself applauding this latest turn of events. He didn't build his namesake behemoth on waste and inefficiency; paring away costs wherever possible is the storied route to Wal-Mart's low customer prices. But Lee Scott goes farther, reminding critics inside the company and out that Walton embraced change when he thought it was the right thing to do for a company that he hoped would outlive him. Walton also loved the outdoors. So putting all the pieces together, Scott is convinced that the Wal-Mart founder would endorse the CEO's shift to sustainability as a way to improve customers' lives, save the planet, and fatten the bottom line.

Raising the Bar to Protect Everyone's Mama

Doing what's right for Mother Nature is the main goal for my colleague Gary Erickson, the founder of Clif Bar, a Berkeley, California–based maker of energy supplements. "She's our mama—let's take care of her," proclaims the company Web site, and Gary is working on several fronts to give Mama her due. For one thing, he's pitching a Global Cooling program aimed at turning down the heat in Mama's kitchen by encouraging people to reduce their use of fossil fuels and to invest in carbon offsets that help build new sources of clean, renewable energy. Having successfully made its own operations carbon-neutral by purchasing renewable energy credits, Clif Bar has set its sights on getting the rest of the world to do the same.

I first met Gary Erickson about six years ago, when I called to see if Clif Bar would be interested in jointly supporting Stonyfield's Strong Women's Summit. Since then, our companies have sponsored hundreds of events together, including the Campus Consciousness Tour. Clif Bars and Stonyfield smoothies go well together, and our teams have formed a bond based on our willingness to take risks on behalf of the planet.

Gary got into the energy food business after nibbling another energy bar over the course of a 175-mile bicycle ride. He came home convinced he could produce something much tastier, and baked his first batch of bars in his mother's kitchen. Now Clif Bar (named for his father) has grown into a 200-person company with annual revenue exceeding $150 million. The company has been profitable since its founding in 1992.

Profits are critical, of course, but if money were the only gauge of success, Gary and his wife, Kit Crawford, would be out of the energy-bar business altogether and living a life of luxury on the millions of dollars they could have made selling out to a big company. It almost happened: In 2000, Gary agreed to sell his business for $120 million. After the rival PowerBar and Balance Bar were bought by Nestlé and Kraft, respectively, Gary feared they would overpower Clif Bar with their newfound advertising clout. (Like Stonyfield, Clif Bar largely depends on grassroots marketing, mainly through its event sponsorships.) But at the last minute, Gary's gut told him he was making a mistake. Companies that get bought "lose their values," he says, which, to his mind, include sustaining your people, your community, and your environment. So he called off the deal.

Gary clearly takes care of his people, and he has a *Fortune* magazine "Best Boss" award to prove it. A walk through Clif Bar's Berkeley headquarters finds employees getting a little exercise in the company gym or on the two-story climbing wall. They bring dogs and dirty laundry to work. The dogs roam free, and the laundry cycles through the washer and dryer installed for the employees' personal use. Massage therapists and hairstylists drop by regularly, and health screenings are done at the office. Clif Bar donates 1 percent of its revenues to community causes each year in the form of cash, volunteer hours, and food. Through the company's employee-run community service program, employees are not only encouraged to volunteer on company time, they are also able to choose the causes and organizations they want to support.

As you might expect from someone who employs an in-house ecologist and a sustainability manager, Gary is committed to a whole range of activities aimed at protecting everyone's Earth mother. For example, Clif Bar:

- Purchases approximately 20 million pounds of organic ingredients each year—70 percent of all the ingredients Clif Bar uses are organic.
- Offsets more than 100 percent of the CO_2 generated by the business's daily operations—including emissions from the office, bakeries, inter-company shipping, and business travel.
- Converted 20,000 miles of annual inter-company shipping to biodiesel.
- Switched secondary cardboard packaging to 100 percent (50 percent post-consumer) recycled paperboard, saving eleven thousand trees and five million gallons of water each year.
- Keeps over 74 percent of office waste out of landfills through its recycling and composting initiatives.
- Uses organically grown cotton and nontoxic inks in its promotional T-shirts.
- Runs its Cool Commute program to reward employees for carpooling, taking public transportation, biking, or walking to work. Clif Bar also offers a $5,000 cash incentive to employees who purchase fuel-efficient hybrid vehicles or cars that run on biodiesel fuel.

But merely making his own business eco-friendly wasn't enough for Gary. His passion for the environment led him to bring others to the cause through Clif Bar's Start Global Cooling program. The idea is to offset greenhouse gas emissions by making investments in clean, renewable energy produced by wind farms.

To help people offset emissions, and hopefully to encourage them to make actual carbon reductions, Clif Bar also sells renewable wind-energy credits in the form of Cool Tags at sponsored events ranging from bike races to music festivals. Each $2 tag purchased from Clif Bar goes to support NativeEnergy's WindBuilders program, which helps to build new Native American- and farmer-owned wind turbines. (That's the same program Stonyfield supports, although there are a number of similar renewable-energy offset programs, including TerraPass and Carbonfund, from which to choose.) For two bucks, the Cool Tag buyer keeps an estimated three hundred pounds of CO_2 from reaching the atmosphere, about what your car belches out of its tailpipe every three hundred miles.

As we have seen, a small but growing number of businesses are rethinking their self-interest—they now realize that reducing carbon pollution can actually be profitable. I'm reminded of Thomas Hardy's words: "If a way to the better there be, it exacts a full look at the worst." These trailblazers have looked at our traditional ways of doing business and seen the worst—the destruction of life itself. They have chosen the better way by voluntarily cleaning up their greenhouse-gas emissions and other pollutants. They fill me with hope for our children's future.

But we're getting ahead of ourselves. In order to clean up a business, you have to have one, and that means attracting customers. Stonyfield has found Earth-friendly ways to do that, too, and the next chapter will show how we and other like-minded companies manage to establish firm bonds of loyalty with our customers.

4

Hands Across the Aisle

Talk about green: We began as totally amateur marketers, handing out yogurt samples from a folding table at a local Stop & Shop with all the innocence of Cub Scouts selling chances for a free car wash. The miracle is that it actually worked. After much trial and error, we achieved what I now call our indispensable handshake with the customer. We did so even more successfully than if Samuel and I had come to the task fully equipped with Harvard MBAs and a brigade of marketing consultants.

We started out with missionary zeal, utterly convinced that the world would love our yogurt. We couldn't imagine otherwise. The yogurt was our faith, our guiding light. The first taste of Stonyfield would melt in our first customer's mouth—then a thousand mouths, then a million, and then more.

Small problem: How would we reach even one mouth? We couldn't afford advertising, so how would anyone hear our gospel, let alone savor our yogurt? How could we possibly demonstrate Stonyfield's proven (at least to us) superiority against whole shelves of rival brands, heavily promoted and firmly entrenched as household names all over America?

Thanks to a family friend, then a Stop & Shop executive, the supermarket chain grudgingly granted us a taste test. We were on the shelves in five stores and allowed to pass out yogurt samples for twelve weeks. We were thrilled. For the first time, we could actually compete with other brands. Or sort of: Our promotional resources were little better than pathetic. We had no cash or credit and only two yogurt demonstrators, Samuel and me, both novices and both already burdened with the necessary ritual of milking our cows twice a day, making the yogurt, and trying to find the money to cover our expenses.

No matter. Armed with chutzpah and a peerless product—victory's essentials—we plunged ahead with our homemade marketing campaign. Usually we took turns, one of us the day's designated milker or supervisor, the other away sales-pitching. In those years, we made only plain yogurt, so we stood at our little table inviting shoppers to sweeten Stonyfield with a drizzle of local maple syrup. Our entire sales kit consisted of the table, a homemade sign, the yogurt, the maple syrup, and one apron.

Some nights, we were lucky enough to cajole Louise Kaymen, Samuel's wife, or a neighbor into milking our cows, so we could join in double-teaming shoppers. I offered a heartfelt sales pitch and a free taste of our yogurt while Samuel slipped a quart container of Stonyfield into each cart, hoping that our solitary product would make it through checkout and into the customer's fridge and permanent taste buds. In essence, we literally relied on word of mouth—taste-pleased mouths. Despite occasional shopper confusion about our company (was Sam and Gary's yogurt connected to Ben & Jerry's ice cream?), we clearly proved that great taste was our key customer hook.

Best of all, we made the indispensable handshake connection with everyone. We literally pressed free samples into every visible palm—shoppers, store operators, dairy managers. The dairy managers especially loved us; they had never seen the owners of a company avidly connecting with one customer at a time. Believe me, it was worth every single long day of milking, driving, and chatting. The payoff was decisive: Within a year, Stop & Shop agreed to sell Stonyfield yogurt in every one of the chain's several hundred supermarkets across New England.

To our taste triumph, we soon added our health appeal. Many yogurt lovers see healthy eating as a cause. When they discovered that Stonyfield was genuinely pure as well as delicious, they couldn't wait to tell like-minded friends. Before long the Stonyfield name was as hot in health-conscious circles as celebrity sins are in supermarket tabloids. All we knew was that our tactics were working. Our market growth was steady and solid. It was also dirt cheap.

In time, we discovered that amusingly outrageous behavior is a sure ticket to free press coverage. For example, once on *The Joe and Andy Show,* the number one morning radio program in Boston, the two hosts bantered about yogurt. It started when Andy, the couch potato, asked Joe, the athletic one, what he was eating.

"Yogurt," came the reply.

You really ought to get healthy, Joe told him and recommended Stonyfield. It was from New Hampshire, Joe said, and it's good for you.

"I'd rather eat camel manure," Andy responded.

I heard about the exchange the next day. So I called our nearby Benson's Animal Farm and made arrangements to pick up frozen camel manure—it was winter. The next morning, on our way to Boston—my wife, Meg, came with me—the manure thawed. We'd let the receptionist at the radio station in on our prank. We had a full quart of Stonyfield yogurt and a container of manure for Andy.

We walked right in, and Andy knew he was trapped. We kept putting a spoonful of manure under Andy's nose. Finally, he tasted the yogurt and made a chewing sound. Then came a long silence.

"Okay," Andy said, "I admit it. This yogurt does taste better than camel manure."

It was our first celebrity product endorsement. What's more, this little caper got us on-air mentions for about three months. Better yet, it intrigued so many listeners that a significant number began adding Stonyfield to their shopping carts. Sales took off—and our only cost was the gas for the drive to Boston.

We learned that brands flourish when they acquire personalities that attract people. Our job was to personalize Stonyfield with friendly gestures—symbolic handshakes—that made customers like us and buy our yogurt. The tactics available to us—or any company for that matter—were and are limited only by imagination.

On another occasion, when we wanted to get into the Chicago market, one of the city's biggest supermarket chains, Dominick's, told us we'd have to capture a 3 percent market share within three months. Otherwise, the chain would pull our product out of its dairy cases.

We were then at 0.8 percent, meaning we had to nearly quadruple our sales in the Chicago market. To get that kind of bang from a conventional advertising buck, we were told, would cost $10 million. Needless to say, we didn't have it. So we rolled out another hand-to-mouth offensive. This time, we zeroed in on public-transport riders, distributing free cups of yogurt on Chicago Metra platforms. The idea was to thank transit riders for saving energy and resources—a message that neatly underlined our basic promise. There was a catch: Food handouts on transit platforms were a no-no. But with a little friendly persuasion from our then vice president of communications, Mary Jo Viederman, we talked the Metra into cutting us some slack. We passed out roughly eighty-five thousand containers of yogurt and spoons, along with coupons that read: "We salute your commute; thanks for doing your part to help save the planet." We also distributed brochures reminding commuters that every person who travels by train instead of car keeps forty-five pounds of particulates per year from spewing into the atmosphere.

All these friendly attention-grabbers got us coverage in every Chicago newspaper, plus the local segment of NBC's *Today* show. And after we had worked those train platforms for only three days, Stonyfield's market share had jumped to nearly 2.5 percent, virtually guaranteeing us a stable position on that chain's shelves. The whole operation cost us only $100,000, or roughly 1 percent of what we would have paid to acquire the same market share through advertising.

The same kind of necessity-driven ingenuity helped us break into the Houston market. We wanted to bond with customers by giving away our yogurt to people who were behaving responsibly and being good to the planet. But Houston, unlike Chicago, is devoid of commuter trains. Cars and pickup trucks rule. Nevertheless, many drivers are very conscious of what fossil-fuel-burning vehicles do to the environment, and they feel a little guilty about it. So we decided to broadcast the fact that if every car's tires were properly inflated, it would increase our nation's fuel efficiency by two miles per gallon of gasoline. The fuel savings would be equivalent to the potential oil production from the Arctic National Wildlife Refuge, and if we could avoid tapping the oil beneath ANWR, a place that is surely better left undisturbed than populated with drilling rigs.

Despite the fact that we were invading oil country, where do-gooding Northerners might be considered no-gooding petrophobes, we headed down to Texas carrying a big sign that said, "We Support Inflation." We set up shop at a busy intersection and posted our placard for all to see. When drivers pulled off the road and into our way station, we pumped up their tires and explained how properly inflated tires could save the wildlife refuge, not to mention a few dollars on gas. Then we gave the drivers a cup of yogurt and a tire gauge emblazoned with the Stonyfield logo, and sent them on their way. As a result, we got a spot on local TV news, reached tens of thousands of commuters, and disseminated our environmental message and product in a nonthreatening way.

But what I've come to realize most clearly about marketing Stonyfield is that winning a customer's attention is only the beginning of a lasting happy relationship. No matter how far we ship our yogurt, whether three miles or three thousand, it's the last eighteen inches—the distance between the yogurt cup and the consumer's mouth—that makes all the difference. Sampling means everything to us. It transforms a contact into a customer, one cup at a time. Put another way, we are a spoonto-mouth brand, and we expand our customer base largely by making an emotional connection with those who sample our product.

And once a connection is formed and the figurative handshake exchanged, we use every customer interaction to strengthen the pact we've made. That means providing high-quality yogurt, doing all we can to protect the environment and promote sustainable farming methods, and living up to our mission to prove that socially and environmentally responsible businesses can still be profitable. Our customers know they can trust us to do what's right for the health and well-being of themselves and their families, our farmer suppliers, and the planet. In short, our contract with the customer is multifaceted and genuine, and it's summed up by the words: "We want you to feel good inside."

For Stonyfield, then, maintaining our side of the bargain means we don't just meet customer expectations; we exceed them. No limp handshake or perfunctory brush of the fingers from us. We press flesh, maintain eye contact, and hold tight to our values. The key is to show an attitude that pleases the customer and makes him or her feel good inside.

The customer's side of this bargain amounts to paying a few extra pennies for a Stonyfield cup of yogurt. We believe that our firm handshake ensures a fair shake, and our customers seem to agree.

"You Can't Fake This Stuff"

I drive our marketing people crazy. I hate advertising. It mostly seems too clever and gimmicky. I consider traditional advertising to be the fertilizer of conventional business. You spray it on a field of consumers to grow their awareness and hopefully incite them to try your product. Then you hope that a trial leads to a purchase, then to repeat purchases, and finally, if you're fortunate, to true product loyalty.

But just as with conventional farming practices, where petroleum-based fertilizer is needed to grow each succeeding year's crops, a fairly high percentage of your revenue has to be plowed back into buying more advertising to keep next year's crop of product users growing. That money thus becomes unavailable for enriching your product and deepening your relationship with the consumers you already have. You're left to depend year after year on what your advertising can deliver. The day that a competitor runs an ad challenging your product, you have only a very thin top layer of customer loyalty to sustain you.

We prefer to invest in a much deeper reservoir of loyalty by putting money and effort into making our customers feel good about us and our product. We support causes that people care about. We invest in educational initiatives that will help them improve and sustain communities and our planet. And even if they don't think that Stonyfield is making their lives better, we believe they will have a sense of well-being that, at some innate level, will connect them to us and our yogurt.

Some years ago, we had one of our typical hand-wringing meetings with Connelly Partners, our Boston advertising agency. For the umpteenth time, we were trying to decide what, if any, advertising we should do and what it should say. And Steve Connelly suddenly blurted, "Damn it, you just can't fake this stuff." Everyone smiled and Steve said, "I think we just nailed it."

He was absolutely right. "You just can't fake this stuff" became our slogan, six simple words that say exactly what Stonyfield is about. And the reason it's so succinct is that it's true—no more words are needed. Even so, effective as the slogan is, we limit our conventional advertising to an absolute minimum and still count on our yogurt-cup lids, unorthodox promotions, and cause-related messages to build our business.

I wouldn't have said so in the early days, but now I believe that lack of traditional advertising has actually worked to our advantage. It makes our customers feel they belong to a special club. Stonyfield doesn't beg anyone to buy our product any more than a club recruits new members via thirty-second television spots. To learn about us and our yogurt, a customer has to be venturesome, alert to new ideas and new tastes, a person who shops for the spices of life, not just another meat loaf. We believe this approach gives us something our competitors lack: incredible customer loyalty, enhanced by our myriad efforts to strengthen our customer bond. Most yogurt brands are indistinguishable. When one is out of stock, grocers tell us, shoppers switch to whatever else is available. But Stonyfield is not a commodity item, not just another yogurt. When it's missing from the dairy case, we're told that people complain.

Educational initiatives are a big part of Stonyfield's campaign to firm up our handshake with customers. We've always stressed both the purity of the food we sell and our larger planet-saving mission. One way we educate is by putting environmental and other important messages on our carton lids—300 million of them every year. In August 2002, for instance, our lids said, "Your car choice makes a difference. Live larger, drive smaller." We change the messages throughout the year, sometimes giving quizzes, or promoting individual causes by discussing issues that threaten our health and the health of the planet, or inviting customers to join the fight by informing them of initiatives by nonprofit environmental groups.

The idea of using our packaging to educate consumers goes back to the very beginning of Samuel's and my yogurt-making careers. One of our earliest quart-size containers carried this message:

> *The Rural Education Center is supported in part by the sale of this yogurt. The center is dedicated to the development of a regional, self-reliant agriculture. Our programs and workshops explore ideas and demonstrate methods that can be used to achieve this goal. We hope our small dairy will be one example of how we can revitalize our agricultural economy. Supporting local agriculture will help assure a healthy and abundant food supply for ourselves and generations to come.*

The back side of the container—this was in the days before nutrition labels took up a big share of space—avowed our "reverence for life" and told our yogurt buyers that Stonyfield cows' diets were free of pesticides and other chemicals, but contained added vitamins, herbs, and "lots of tender loving care." In 1989, after I was already working and living at Stonyfield, I realized that small cups were the wave of the future, and the lids were an obvious billboard for our message.

The power of our lids can be used in many ways. A few years back, we printed one that customers could send to their representatives in Congress. It said: "I believe in efficient government, but not at the expense of my children's future. If you vote against the planet, I won't vote for you." Dick Gephardt, then the House Democratic leader, told me that fifteen thousand of those lids made their way to Capitol Hill.

Another aspect of our customer handshake is our Web site, Stonyfield.com. It's loaded with information about everything we do, including our support for organic family farming and our pledge to return 10 percent of each year's profit to environmental causes. Kids love the "Have a Cow" program that lets them become make-believe part-owners of cows on our supplier farms. Since we started the program in 1989, hundreds of thousands of people have learned about farm life through the quarterly updates posted on the Web site or e-mailed to them by their unusually articulate bovine friends.

When you join the program, you download a photo and the biography of a real cow, and the quarterly reports tell about her life and what's happening on the farm. We hope to give people an idea of what farm life is really like, how dairy farming works, and some of the challenges farmers face. Here, for instance, is part of a dispatch from Hershey, a calf on the Choiniere family farm:

> Born November 7, 2006, I'm still a very spunky calf! I got my name because I'm half Jersey and half Holstein, and if you look closely at my picture you can see I'm neither black and white like a Holstein nor honey-brown like a Jersey; instead I'm brown and white.
>
> I live with the rest of the calves in an area that is attached to the back of the milking barn. Out here I enjoy kicking my hooves up, high into the air, and running around my pen with

my friends. When Hannah or Mathieu come to clean my pen, I follow them around trying to suck on their clothes.

For the first 2 months or so, I drank warm milk twice a day. Hannah fed me my milk, making sure the temperature was perfect—when milk comes out of a cow it is 101 degrees. She fed me 3 quarts of milk, twice a day.

Did you know a cow has 4 stomachs? They are the rumen, omasum, reticulum, and abomasum. These compartments can also be found in other ruminant animals such as buffalo, elephants, deer, camels, and kangaroos. Ruminants are able to digest high quantities of roughage, something that no other animal can do.

The rumen is the largest compartment of the stomach. When a cow is eating or grazing, all of her food goes into the rumen first. In the rumen there are enzymes that help break down the food so the nutrients can be absorbed into the body. . . .

. . . At birth, my rumen is very small and undeveloped. As I start to eat grain and hay, my stomach starts to grow and become active. By the time I'm six to nine months old, my rumen will be completely functioning very much like my mother's. Can you believe she can hold up to 100 pounds of feed in her rumen! For now, I'll eat organic aloe pellets, milk, and Hannah's clothes.

Yes, the kids reading that are likely to groan, "Eewww, gross!" But they're also sure to remember it—and they'll know a lot more than they did before about the fascinating facts of nature, farm life, and our planet. Our bet is that, in the long run, that's good for the kids, for all people on Earth, and for Stonyfield, too.

I don't mean to suggest that Stonyfield's marketing practices are unique, and you certainly don't have to be a yogurt company to succeed by adapting our methods. Companies of all kinds can and have triumphed using unconventional approaches. The one you're about to meet, for instance, took an unusual idea, married it to an equally unorthodox marketing campaign bolstered by a planet-healing mission, and turned the whole shebang into a solidly profitable and growing business. This is the first of this chapter's case studies in the art of great handshakes, the powerful gestures that cement deep, honest, and lasting relationships with loyal customers.

Zipcar's Un-American Triumph

Zipcar is a company built on a premise so unconventional that it seems, at first glance, almost un-American: You don't have to own a car to get where you're going. You can share cars with other drivers, who will use them when you don't need them. Unlikely as this may sound in a country that cherishes solo car-owning, Zipcar's skill at selling sharing has forged a handshake with customers that may well presage some kind of social revolution.

Back in 2000, when the first Zipcars appeared in and around Boston, the company's offbeat notion faced an uphill battle just to win believers, let alone succeed. After all, owning a car is part of being a grown-up in this country. Never mind that the average car is driven less than an hour a day. Or that it costs roughly $700 a month to own a car, when you add up the cost of gas, insurance, depreciation, repairs, and parking fees.

Or that driving thirty hours in a Zipcar would cost less than $300, saving you $400 a month, enough to finance an annual vacation in Hawaii. And how about the fact that car owners are stuck with the same car on every trip, whether they're going out on a date or lugging a sofa home from Ikea? Never mind all that. In large part, our cars define our identities: We are what we drive.

But why? wondered Robin Chase and Antje Danielson. Danielson had just vacationed in Berlin and seen car sharing—cars parked around town for members to drive by the hour, an arrangement that has been common in Europe for two decades. After all, the two friends reasoned, you don't have to own a refinery to get gasoline, or a slaughterhouse to get beef. Sharing cars would be convenient, especially for city dwellers, and it would spread the costs of ownership, saving substantial sums of money for the lucky members.

And, in short order, Zipcars appeared. These days, they're waiting in garages or parking lots dotted around dozens of metropolitan areas, within walking distance of prospective customers. To use them, members phone or go online to make a reservation. They find their cars in the designated spots and wave their plastic Zipcards over the windshields, at which point the computers inside compare the cards with the reservations, unlock the doors, and tell the ignition that it can respond to the key dangling by the steering wheel. Insurance is paid, repairs are taken care of, and if the driver needs gas, there's a Zipcar credit card in the glove compartment. The cost: $8.50 an hour and up, depending on the model.

Like Stonyfield Farm, the fledgling Zipcar had a planet-saving cause to bolster its appeal: Sharing cars would ease highway congestion and the parking crunch; members would use the cars more sparingly when paying by the hour, thus cutting down total emissions and helping the environment. But in the early days, it was still a foreign concept and a hard sell.

Also like Stonyfield, CEO Robin Chase and her successor Scott Griffith had little money for advertising. And when Chase tried it anyway, it proved of little use. Brand recognition improved, but few real people applied for the $25 membership. So Zipcar turned to tactics that, in essence, built handshakes with customers.

If you're in the business of renting cars, you don't automatically think of city governments as natural allies. But the environmental case for car sharing, though slow to catch on with drivers, had a direct appeal in city halls. Zipcar's statistics showed that every car available for sharing takes fifteen to twenty cars off the road, reducing the need to build highways and add parking spaces.

In London, Zipcar worked with Transport for London to create the city's on-street car sharing program, dedicating coveted curb parking spaces solely to car-sharing vehicles. The Washington Metropolitan Area Transit Authority (WMATA) in Washington, D.C., has Zipcars waiting at downtown and suburban stations, allowing travelers to use rapid transit and finish their trips by Zipcar. And Greenbelt, Maryland, has a Zipcar at a senior citizens' complex for subsidized rent to residents at just $1 an hour.

Clogged as they are with students' cars, universities provided another target for Zipcar's offbeat marketing. After Wellesley College in the Boston suburbs made Zipcars available to all its students, dozens of other universities followed suit—making it possible to crack down on parking violations and tighten restrictions for car permits on campus.

Scott Griffith found that most of his customers were using Zipcars in evenings and on weekends. Looking to fill the idle hours, he extended the company's handshake to corporations. When companies found they could downsize or even sell off the corporate fleet and save thousands in vehicle costs, repairs, insurance, and parking fees, Griffith's Z2B program quickly took off, with hundreds of businesses joining within the first year.

And it was Griffith who discovered the power of customer handshaking for Zipcar. He calls it zone marketing, zeroing in on individual neighborhoods where Zipcars are available, and especially on neighborhoods where Zipcars are just being introduced. Since the key to getting them used is having enough available, Zipcar moves into a new territory with a lot of cars and alerts prospective customers on where to find them. There are Zipcar posters at restaurants and movie theaters, and stacks of brochures in ice cream parlors and on bank counters. Zipcar employees hand out cards to people getting off buses and subway trains, set up booths at street markets and community fairs, and occasionally park outside the Whole Foods Market and offer carless shoppers a free ride home with their groceries. The resulting buzz in the neighborhood inevitably lures experimental users and often gets media attention. In Boston, a reporter wrote that he had tried the service for five months and always found a car within walking distance when he needed one. The free publicity was good evidence that Zipcar's customer handshake was strong and healthy.

Where Zipcar does use advertising, it has an even jauntier tagline than Stonyfield's "You can't fake this stuff." One Zipcar ad proclaims, "350 hours/year having sex. 420 looking for parking. What's wrong with this picture?"

What's right with Zipcar's picture is the power of marketing with well-aimed empathy (aka handshaking). The company got inside the heads of young, carless city dwellers, spotted their unfilled need, and filled it economically and efficiently. Zipcar also respects its customers' tastes: no dreary black Malibus or white Taurus sedans for this crowd. Zipcars range from BMWs to sporty Mini Coopers, from Toyota's hybrid Prius to Ford SUVs. And the business is clearly scalable. The company now has more than three thousand cars in dozens of North American cities, including Ann Arbor, Boston, Chicago, Chapel Hill, Minneapolis, New York, San Francisco, Toronto, Vancouver, and Washington, D.C., as well as London, England. Growing at a rate of 100 percent a year, it recently raised another $25 million during its second round of institutional funding—money raised to expand operations in existing markets and expand services in North America and Europe. By 2010, it plans to offer Zipcars in twenty-five major metropolitan markets and half a dozen more European cities.

Zipcar exemplifies the advantages of handshaking—of marketing with a mission that appeals to significant groups of like-minded people. The same goes for Seventh Generation, a cleaning-products company based in Burlington, Vermont. But Seventh Generation is subjecting the concept to a very hard test. Unlike Zipcar, which has the stage largely to itself, Seventh Generation is going head-to-head with some of America's biggest, most traditional cleaning-products manufacturers.

Yet, it's gaining ground. How? By building its customer handshake with serious ecological education, a sort of mind-shake.

Seventh Generation Greens Up Mr. Clean

Move aside, Mr. Clean. Mr. Green is muscling in on your housekeeping business and showing off his skill as an eco-friendly dirt-buster. Fueled by government and parental concerns over how household chemicals are affecting children's health and well-being, the market for natural cleaning products is beginning to bubble. According to the Organic Trade Association, sales of nontoxic cleaning agents have tripled in the past five years. Market researchers say that an arresting 84 percent of all U.S. consumers are now interested in green cleaning options.

This news from the home front is thrilling for my friend Jeffrey Hollender, the founder, president, and chief executive officer of Seventh Generation, the fastest-growing brand of natural household and personal care products in the United States. For the last five years Seventh Generation has grown 30 to 40 percent and this year, sales will reach almost $100 million. Jeffrey has been working since Seventh Generation's founding in 1988 to foment a nontoxic cleaning-product revolution. He's even written a book about it: *Naturally Clean—Seventh Generation's Guide to Safe & Healthy Non-Toxic Cleaning.*

What Jeffrey and Seventh Generation haven't done is to rely on traditional advertising to get their message out to consumers. Instead, the company has built its handshake with customers by designing and formulating natural products that people want, educating consumers about the benefits of its environmental stance, forming strong bonds with them through a host of company-led initiatives, and nurturing a robust network of national distributors.

Seventh Generation started as a mail-order business selling energy-conservation products. Its current mission is more dynamic. The company is named for—and driven by—an Iroquois belief that, in making any decision, tribal leaders should pay heed to the impact their actions will have at least seven generations hence. Jeffrey and his company have applied that precept to business decisions. The goal is to make sure that every time a customer uses a Seventh Generation product, he or she is making a safer and better world for those who come after—by saving natural resources, cutting back on pollutants, and preventing toxic chemicals from harming the environment and their own health.

To that end, the company is moving away from making products that are simply less harmful than those made by mainstream competitors. It is now aggressively focused on truly eco-friendly products. Among other things, it pressures suppliers to be environmentally and socially responsible. To keep Seventh Generation's business, its suppliers have to match the company's own standards, including public disclosure of how well or badly it carries out its corporate responsibilities.

Seventh Generation also believes that a major part of its mission is to educate consumers, inspiring them to help foster "environmental sustainability, social justice, and compassion for all living creatures." Just as we do at Stonyfield, Seventh Generation uses its packaging, its Web site, and the CEO's books and audience presentations to spread its message. It publishes a monthly e-newsletter, *The Non-Toxic Times*. And in a nod to today's social-networking craze, it also sponsors a blog site, InspiredProtagonist.com.

Consumer questions and concerns are addressed on the company's Web site—questions, for example, about the health and environmental effects of chlorine, petroleum, and other ingredients found in commonly used household cleaners. Seventh Generation estimates that the average home contains three to ten gallons of bleach, ammonia, and other toxic ingredients found in assorted cleaning products, only a fraction of which have been judged safe for humans to use. Astonishingly enough, many chemicals used routinely in household products are banned in the workplace by the Occupational Health and Safety Administration.

Clicking on the site's "Living Green" section takes you to Seventh Generation's complete line of goods—including chlorine-free bleach, diapers, baby wipes, and feminine-care products; phosphate-free cleaning and laundry products; and 100 percent-recycled paper towels, tissues, and napkins. The products carry descriptions of their eco-friendly characteristics and their superior ability to do the jobs they are made to do.

The Non-Toxic Times is full of environmental news and views intended to educate and motivate readers. In the February 2007 issue, for instance, the lead article recounted Jeffrey's decision to switch over to a "Greasecar," a vehicle converted to run on clean-burning recycled cooking oil. Admitting that he'd love to tool around Vermont in a spiffy new convertible, Jeffrey explains that his conscience won't allow it in an era of "overconsumption, global warming, dirty air, and other earthly maladies." Instead, he's settled on "a used 1983 Mercedes diesel station wagon" that lumbers around smelling "like a large order of fries." Aromas aside, Jeffrey writes, his Greasecar allows him to save about 550 gallons of gasoline each year and keep 6,500 pounds of carbon emissions out of the atmosphere.

What Jeffrey loves best about his Greasecar is the positive reaction it gets. Whether he talks to truck drivers, urban professionals, or college kids, everyone says the car is cool—a wheeled billboard touting all the right stuff for our time, notably energy independence and environmental sanity. "I actually feel proud every time I get behind the wheel," Jeffrey says.

The same commitment is also evident in the company's Inspired Protagonist blog. Here the goal is to build a lively community of change agents, eager to recruit others for environmental action. As Jeffrey recently explained to a *Financial Times* reporter, Seventh Generation is really selling a worldview, not a product.

The proof that Seventh Generation's message is being heard is found in its remarkable growth. The company's clean green household and personal care products are showing up in more and more stores, including big chains like Albertson's, Kroger, and Target, as well as numerous online venues.

Meanwhile, consumer perceptions are clearly changing and Seventh Generation's much bigger rivals are having to adjust their business practices as a result. Procter & Gamble, Kimberly-Clark, SC Johnson, and the like have been forced to be more transparent about what goes into their products. SC Johnson, the maker of ubiquitous staples including Windex and Fantastik, has responded to growing consumer concerns by taking the ammonia out of new product recipes—while, of course, still defending the ammonia-laden versions as totally "safe."

A nice gesture on Johnson's part, perhaps, but, as Seventh Generation sees it, the problems go much deeper than ammonia. A recent edition of the company newsletter pointed out that persistent organic pollutants (POPs—the term refers to chlorinated hydrocarbon chemicals that are found in pesticides, household and industrial chemicals, and manufacturing and waste by-products) have been linked to some of the world's worst health problems, including cancer, reproductive maladies, hormonal disorders, and possibly, based on the results of a Korean study, the growing scourge of diabetes.

Getting this kind of information into the hands of consumers and giving them a chance to discuss it on the blog site—and, hopefully, to act on it—cements the company's relationship with its customers in a way that no thirty-second advertising spot ever could. Consumers themselves become foot soldiers in the fight that Jeffrey and his company are helping to lead.

More to the point, Jeffrey is acutely aware that accepting environmental and social responsibility is a big part of his handshake with his customers. As he told a Greenpeace interviewer, "You generally make more money when you do the right thing. When you do the wrong thing, people sue you, governments fine you, sales plunge, disgusted employees sabotage you, community groups start picketing, reporters show up. . . . And, ultimately . . . pollution is waste; waste represents inefficiency; and inefficiency is simply not profitable. It's that simple."

Zipcar and Seventh Generation have built handshakes with their customers by meeting not only their product needs, but also, in effect, their emotional needs. These companies seem unusually aware of the universal search for meaning in an often meaningless world. I applaud their acumen.

Other companies may build handshakes with their customers based on all sorts of social concerns, and more power to them. My own concern is the urgent need to help my customers and everyone else to grasp just how critical the entwined concepts of sustainability and efficiency are to the health of our only planet. The next chapter tells how Stonyfield and some of its colleagues have fomented, and benefited from, the organic food revolution.

5

The Delicious Revolution

In the early days, organic food was often a grueling experience that required a lot of chewing. To the faithful few, it nourished a feeling of virtue, of salivation, as it were. To the skeptical many, it was a burp of ideology at the expense of taste and texture.

I remember one Thanksgiving at the New Alchemy Institute when my family came to visit. My housemate, Rob, had made an organic pumpkin soup for us before leaving to spend the holiday with his own family. The soup was awful. After one spoonful, I declared my innocence in this culinary crime and tossed out the evidence. "If this is organic food," my mother chimed in, "bring on the chemicals." Fortunately, the organic salad, yams, and turkey were delicious, and by the end of the dinner, Mom had come around.

Organic isn't just about food. It's a much more expansive way of thinking that embraces cyclical, nonlinear resource use, where waste from one activity becomes food for another. It honors natural laws and it abhors the mindless dispersal of toxic chemicals. Cheap substitutes don't work. That's why you can't replace organic farming with chemical farming and expect anything but depleted soil, poor crops, and unstable prices.

The skeptics say that organic isn't proven yet. But I say it's chemicals that aren't proven. All of humanity ate organic food until the early part of the twentieth century. We've been on a chemical binge diet for about eighty years—an eyeblink in planetary history—and what do we have to show for it? We've lost one-third of America's original topsoil, buried toxic waste everywhere, polluted and depleted water systems, worsened global warming, and exacerbated ailments ranging from cancer to diabetes to obesity.

This is not airy blather touting the tofu way to happiness. I see organic as part of a philosophy of wholeness, the science of integration, the need to keep nature humming as the interdependent web of life. Organic is also a pragmatic state of mind, offering real antidotes to society's assorted ills and errors. It backs a sensible farm policy that protects not only family farmers, but also the health of all Americans—when you eat better, you are better. In fact, an organic food system could bring down health-care costs by eliminating toxic lifestyles and the unnecessary disease and illness they cause.

Organic methods of agriculture can help stabilize fuel prices and reduce our dependence on foreign oil. They can lead to true national security, which, in turn, fosters planetary security. By using less fossil fuel and chemicals, and by trapping and building carbon in the soil instead of in the atmosphere, organic farming is a crucial WME (weapon of mass enlightenment) in humanity's now-or-never fight against the air pollution that causes global warming. In short, there's nothing "alternative" about organic.

Back in the 1970s, organic food had no such positive image. Many dismissed it as a fringy fad served cold with an eat-your-spinach sermon. How could organic taste good? Indeed, taste was the key challenge. Organic advocates couldn't popularize a cuisine simply by declaring it spiritually and ecologically superior. The world, like my mother, was not waiting for or willing to eat inedible soul food. To win acceptance, it had to be truly delectable.

But that would take a while. Many of us had gotten involved in the organic movement for political reasons—to protest industrial agriculture. Some of us were back-to-the-land rebels with a strong passion for eating locally grown food. Others were food purists, excited by the opportunity to propagate and preserve heirloom varieties of produce and seed stocks. Still others came to the cause simply for the joy of growing our own food.

What began as a philosophical fondness for dishes like brown rice and seaweed eventually matured into a tasty cuisine that attracted talented chefs, notably my friend Alice Waters, who called organics "the delicious revolution." The title of this chapter is my tribute to her.

In those early days, many of us felt that our passion, in all its various forms, could bloom into businesses—if "we" grew it, "they" would buy. But that was a misjudgment that spawned lots of bankruptcies. I was committed to both the food and the politics, but I also believed that if organics were to gain traction and grow beyond our original small enclave of activists, America's supermarkets—and, more important, the way they did business—would have to be accommodated. Inevitably, this led to friction with various friends who seemed more interested in fighting culture wars than seizing new commercial opportunities. I let them go their way, and never really looked back.

On some level, I sensed that it was only a matter of time before the world came around to the diverse business possibilities of the organic way of life. But even I couldn't have foreseen back then just how huge and profitable the opportunity would become.

Today, burgeoning demand for organic food is winning over some of the biggest names in retailing, including Safeway, Kroger, Costco, Target, Publix, H-E-B, and others—even Wal-Mart, which is nothing if not savvy about where to make money. It's exciting to think of price-conscious shoppers the world over voting with their pocketbooks to save the Earth.

Stonyfield Farm's Organic Growth

In Stonyfield's early days, the notion of organic going mainstream was only a dream. We faced immediate problems of supply and demand: We didn't have much of either. Sure, a few farm cooperatives were growing and selling organic products to a few buyers. But the vast majority of milk producers and consumers weren't remotely interested. We compromised, using natural ingredients such as hormone-free milk, but without imposing other restrictions on our suppliers.

The organic milk market finally began to churn in the early 1990s. The precipitating move came when Monsanto went a bridge too far in its biotech invasion of the food market: After years and millions of dollars spent on lobbying, and despite the testimony of nutrition and agriculture experts including myself, Monsanto won official approval to sell its bovine growth hormone, rBST, for use in milk cattle. Adding to the outrage, Monsanto also successfully lobbied the FDA so that companies would not have to disclose that milk came from hormone-injected cows. This was what made Horizon Organic Dairy and the Organic Valley Family of Farms launch large-scale organic production. It was also the trigger for my own decision to make Stonyfield fully organic.

We got another break when Peter and Bunny Flint abandoned conventional dairy farming to launch their Organic Cow brand in Tunbridge, Vermont. We began working with the Flints in 1994, buying the milk we needed to convert our plain, whole-milk yogurt from natural to organic, first in a one-quart container and then in six-ounce cups. It was a gamble from the first spoonful, because our yogurt was already pricier than every other conventional brand and the cost would have to increase even further. Having committed ourselves to keeping a high floor price for organic milk, we had to price Stonyfield yogurt high enough to cover the expense of paying the Flints and our other suppliers a hefty premium over conventionally produced milk. And when we added fruit and sugar to the mix, our production costs rose still higher. Like milk, organically grown sugar and fruit were priced twice as high as conventional ingredients.

Fortunately, our customers did not flinch. They kept paying our price for six ounces of our organic yogurt, even though they could buy eight ounces of a conventional brand for the same price. Of course, we were, in a sense, stealing from Peter to pay Paul, since our own nonorganic natural products (then 90 percent of our business) were subsidizing the switch to organic.

At the time, I wondered if I was risking the company's future. But by 2001, our volume was rising and our costs were dropping, with organic sugar on its way to price parity with conventionally grown sweetener in 2003. The unbeatable combination of growth and savings kept us alive and steered us to prosperity.

By 2007, we converted the last 15 percent of our products to organic. Being "natural" is a good thing, but despite all the talk about natural foods these days, we still lack tough standards defining exactly what the term means for consumers. Moreover, my big concern is that farmers raising natural food crops have no guarantee they'll be fairly compensated, regardless of how much time and money they spend protecting the Earth.

Organic Is as Organic Does

The organic food business is the only industry I know that actively seeks increased government regulation. It's our way of remedying public confusion about the meaning of organic. In 1979, the need for clear standards led my partner Samuel to form the Natural Organic Farming Association (now the Northeast Organic Farming Association), the first of many private and state agencies that eventually certified farms and foods as truly organic. In turn, the need to clarify local disparities led

Congress to pass a federal law ordering the U.S. Department of Agriculture (USDA) to create a single set of nationwide standards.

Completed in 2002, those criteria strictly define three levels of organic labeling. The term "100% Organic" is fairly self-explanatory, and refers to foods and fibers that are indeed produced organically at every step, from farm field to store shelf. The second level, simply "Organic," requires that at least 95 percent of a product's ingredients be organic, with the remaining 5 percent strictly limited to ingredients on USDA's National List of Allowable and Prohibited Materials. To certify our vanilla yogurt as organic, for example, inspectors must inspect and certify multiple supply sources—the farms producing our organic milk, sugar, and vanilla beans, and the company turning the beans into our vanilla extract—along with our own Yogurt Works. The third category, "Made with Organic," means that at least 70 percent of a product's ingredients are organic.

The upshot is that the word "organic" is more credible than ever. But I still wish consumers were given more exacting data about the nutritional content and benefits of all their foods. Knowing more about how the food we buy is produced might shake otherwise heedless consumers and get them asking questions about many conventional food-growing methods. Maybe they would want to know just what kind of food and antibiotics were pumped into the animals that end up as beef steaks, pork chops, and chicken tenders on our tables. Or perhaps they would be interested to learn which pesticide was sprayed on their fruits and vegetables, along with its potential health effects. Cheaper at the checkout might not seem like such a bargain if the longer-term consequences were more readily apparent. As it is, too many consumers are lulled into complacency by a lack of meaningful information.

Organic food is already a $17.7 billion-a-year business in the United States. Given the market's steady growth, mainline food companies have lately hastened to acquire or create their own organic brands, among them Frito-Lay's organic Tostitos brand tortilla chips and salsa, Heinz Organic Tomato Ketchup, and Kellogg's Organic Raisin Bran, Rice Krispies, and Mini-Wheats cereals. My wife, Meg, recently discovered organic Raisin Bran on our supermarket's shelves. Had she told me ten years ago that Kellogg's sold an organic cereal, I would have thought she was delusional.

With the likes of Wal-Mart and Target putting pressure on organic suppliers to watch prices, and with companies like Frito-Lay, Kellogg's, and Heinz joining the competition, some of my organic colleagues worry that we will lose our ability to charge a premium and be forced to start undermining farmers' prices, along with quality and standards. But I welcome the trend. There is no denying that the turn toward organic products is a big plus for America's health and our planet's environment. If the good stuff becomes commoditized, and if entrepreneurs continually raise the bar by adding in extra nutrition, there will be less bad stuff on the market and less strain on our environment. And isn't that our ultimate goal? If we are really committed to saving the world, we'll stop questioning motives and start applauding every big company that makes the effort to change course and embrace organic methods.

Various large corporations are buying their way into the

organic market by acquiring established players—and sadly, many of them are weakening and diluting these brands (although, fortunately, that's not the case with Groupe Danone, which holds an 85 percent interest in Stonyfield Farm). Anyone with enough money can buy a company, but it takes a real commitment to the core principles of organic farming and business methods to nurture it and make it work.

Kellogg's, for instance, has successfully grown its Kashi brand of healthy, natural, whole-grain products to some fifty items, and now has expanded its organic line of cereals to the mainline Kellogg's brand.

I look forward to the day when organic foods are ubiquitous, but it's a long way off. Right now, despite healthy growth, organics' U.S. market penetration is still a mere 2.5 percent. To look at it another way, organic business opportunities abound. All we need are creative entrepreneurs.

With the big players come economies of scale that should eventually nudge the prices of organic products closer to conventional items on supermarket shelves without doing so on the backs of farmers. I expect the gap to narrow to perhaps 8 to 10 percent from an average 20 percent premium now. Still, organic food will probably never be as cheap as the conventional kind. On the other hand, thanks to standards with teeth, organic will be real food.

Even so, my hunch is that this price disparity will become ever more acceptable as more people realize that we have no real knowledge about what happens to our kids' bodies when they grow up on foods containing animal hormones, antibiotics, and pesticide residues. As the toxins accumulate, what are the long-term effects? Do they cause cancer or other lethal diseases?

Such questions lead me to suggest that organic food is one of those rare products that actually gives you far more than you pay for.

Consider what this means for every one of us: The fact is that food, the staple of life, our most basic need, can be vastly improved by goodwill, know-how, and organic practices. But how do we get this truth across to millions? How do we pierce America's 24/7 cacophony of artificially sweet commercials touting fake foods that stuff young bodies with hollow calories?

The Manure Is the Message

I keep experimenting with new ways to get out the organic message. For example, we recently looked at our advertising budget and extracted the dollars needed to launch a cross-country tour that educates America's citizens about organic methods and benefits. The idea is to reach about a million people with an amusing experience that, instead of just showing Stonyfield in a thirty-second television spot, creates an emotional connection to us.

In Chicago parks, we set up a mobile farm exhibit centered around a big, fiberglass Jersey milk cow. Every ten minutes, the cow pooped out organic potting soil instead of manure. We put the soil in a bucket and carried it to a worktable where the kids hand-mixed it and learned what it's good for. The kids loved the show, and the *Chicago Tribune* promptly ran a second-page story on us with a photograph of our cow.

We've since taken the show to dozens of cities. All we're doing is illustrating what happens in nature every single day, but we're doing it with a little humor. The kids take the potting soil/manure and pack it into little pots made from plastic recycled from Stonyfield yogurt containers. We give them organic seeds to plant in the pots, and they go home to watch their organic plants germinate and grow. Believe it or not, our road show has generated e-mail fan letters. Meanwhile, we've increased organic awareness and built brand loyalty to boot, which is good for our bottom line.

And we are not alone. Like Stonyfield, the companies I've chosen to highlight in this book are committed to doing business the organic way. Most important, they all happen to make superior products. Honest Tea is a perfect example. It pays a premium for superior ingredients and minimizes marketing to help offset its higher production costs. What drives its founders, though, is maintaining the quality of their finished product. That's why Honest Tea is a consistent winner for both its taste and its organic purity.

Honest Tea Is the Best Policy

Seth Goldman and Barry Nalebuff knew exactly what they wanted: a refreshing, healthy drink with an only slightly sweet taste. After much tinkering, they invented a tasty brew they rightly called Honest Tea. When they made it organic as well as delicious, their business boiled over, and they pleased palates across the country. Honest Tea now claims two-thirds of all sales in the organic bottled-tea market. In business for less than a decade, the brand was headed for $25 million in revenue in 2007. In 2005, its sales jumped by an awesome 67 percent, followed in 2006 by a nearly equal amount. Meanwhile, the $47 billion carbonated soft-drink business is shrinking by 2 percent a year, despite all its marketing know-how and the vast sums spent on advertising. Honest Tea has set a goal of nearly doubling its sales to $40 million by 2008. The company has attracted media attention and assorted honors, such as the 2003 Dream Big award given by Visa Business and *Inc.* magazine. In 2006, *Consumer Reports* named Honest Tea the top bottled tea.

The Honest Tea story is a rarity in the beverage business, where launching a brand from scratch is a risky and usually failing venture. For all its marketing muscle, even Coca-Cola couldn't break into the black with its fledgling Fruitopia a few years back. What Honest Tea has going for it is its organic purity, its fresh, appealing flavors, and the fact that in everything it does, the company strives to live up to its name.

Full disclosure: Stonyfield has invested $5.9 million in Honest Tea; I sit on its board; I count Seth and Barry among my friends. So I'm not exactly unbiased about the company. But reading this brief account will persuade you that these guys know a secret: An organic product, coupled with authenticity and integrity, is a proven path to bottom- and top-line business growth.

The story begins in 1995, when Barry was teaching at the Yale School of Management (he's still there) and Seth was his star student. They were discussing a study of bottled drinks when they noticed an odd fact: Except for bottled water, every nonalcoholic drink on the market—fruit juices, iced teas, sodas—was saturated with high-fructose corn syrup, the equivalent of a dozen teaspoons of sugar in a twelve-ounce can or bottle.

Seth and Barry both looked in vain for a drink that wasn't overly sweet, and they agreed that here was a conspicuous gap in the beverage business. Surely they weren't the only thirsty Americans who disliked liquid candy. They promised each other, only half in jest, that someday they would form a company to sell their own ideal drink—truly refreshing, lightly sweetened.

Flash forward two years. Seth has been working at the Calvert Group of socially responsible mutual funds, and Barry has been traveling in India. Fresh from a run in New York's Central Park, Seth is frustrated all over again when he and a friend try to find something to kill their thirst. Seth calls Barry and asks, "Did you ever do anything with that idea? Because I'm ready to." "No," says Barry, "but now I'm ready to help make it happen."

In India, Barry had discovered tea—or rather, the economics of tea. His previous thinking about lightly sweetened drinks had focused on mixing juices, perhaps orange or cranberry, with seltzer or club soda, but that would have been dauntingly costly. At a tea auction in India, he learned that just like fine wines, truly good tea is a hundred times as expensive as the dregs of the market—but even the best tea costs just pennies a glass. The kind of tea used in most American bottled teas is the lower quality fannings left over when all the better tea has been sold to more discriminating drinkers. In fact, the American bottlers actually need the most bitter, astringent tea in order to retain any taste when mixed with all that high-fructose corn syrup.

To Barry, the basic proposition was clear: If he used really good tea, it would cost only cents more per bottle than rival teas or soft drinks, and that added cost would be offset by using much less sweetening. He could use organic sugar, too—maybe even honey or maple syrup. Promising fewer calories and better quality, the drink could compete head-on with mass-marketed beverages, and would probably command a premium price from health-conscious customers. It would be genuine, unadulterated, the real thing—and with that, the name came to him: Honest Tea.

When Seth heard all this, he signed on as Tea-EO. He quit his job, and he and Barry, as chairman of the company, raised $500,000 from family and friends to start the business. They began experimenting, brewing one kind of tea after another for friends, students, and colleagues to taste. They settled on five fairly exotic varieties and hired a focus group to try them out.

The next epiphany came when one of the tasters, sipping a green tea with roasted rice called Genmaicha, blurted out, "I know you're paying me to drink this, but do I have to?" Seth and Barry realized that Americans were in the early stages of tea appreciation, and these exotic blends were too far ahead of their market. So they added such flavors as mint, lemongrass, and blood orange to make their brews more compatible with American tastes. They also gave their flavors memorable names: Community Green, Peach Oo-la-long, Just Black.

The big break came when Seth, armed with five thermoses of tea and an empty Snapple bottle with a cobbled-up Honest Tea label, made a sales call on a company named Fresh Fields. When Fresh Fields, which has since become part of the Whole Foods Market chain, ordered fifteen thousand bottles, Seth managed to conceal his terror about how he would actually produce that much. Honest Tea was in business.

It was indeed difficult to find a manufacturer. For one thing, actual tea leaves are much harder to handle on a production line than the concentrates and syrups that other brands use. What's more, Seth and Barry insisted on brewing their tea just as connoisseurs do, with freshly boiled water and loose leaves. They finally found a plant to do the work in Pennsylvania.

From the beginning, Seth and Barry knew theirs would be an unconventional kind of business. Hence the name Honest Tea—and a world-changing optimism that Seth expressed in the company's first label designs. The label on the back of the bottle included a small circle with a tree inside and the words "plant a tree." When Barry asked what it meant exactly, all Seth could say was that he envisioned their business as planting the seeds of hope for a more beautiful future—something that might not blossom fully in their lifetimes.

Seth and Barry clearly had organic souls, but in the early days, organically grown tea was hard to find. With so little apparent demand for organic, Asia's big tea producers saw no reason to stop using pesticides and chemical fertilizers. Still, Honest Tea was able to bring out its first organic brand, First Nation Peppermint, in February 1999, one year after the company's launch and eight months after its first bottles of tea landed on store shelves. It was made with organic mint supplied by a woman-owned company on the Crow Indian reservation in Montana, and Seth and Barry were proud of and excited by their partnership with the Native American community. Here was a chance to help an economically struggling group develop a rewarding business that respected the tribe's traditions and cultural identity.

Then came a fortuitous crisis for tea drinkers. In a series of exposés, European media revealed that tea—most of which is grown in India, China, Kenya, Sri Lanka, Indonesia, Turkey, and Japan—was full of pesticide residues. Tea drinkers discovered to their horror, Seth told me, that tea leaves don't get rinsed; they are simply picked and then dried. "The first time any chemicals on the leaves are washed off is when hot water is poured on them to make tea, so the chemicals end up in the teacup." Demand in Europe plummeted. With that, major planters began switching to organic methods. By 2003, all the tea used in Honest Tea brands was organic, but it took the company another couple of years to switch over to all-organic ingredients. Honest Tea now sells twenty-four flavors of organic tea and Honest Ade fruit drinks in several flavors.

Making the business case for organic tea was fairly easy, Seth told me. It appeals to the growing segment of health-conscious consumers. Ten years ago, people bought organic because they wanted to save the Earth, Seth says. Now they want to save themselves—and that's a pretty powerful purchase motivator. The rigid organic discipline is a natural draw for the health-conscious, offering as it does what Seth describes as reassuring "third-party oversight" for people seeking a cleaner product.

Honest Tea's operations are inspected at every step along the way, from tea gardens to bottling plant, by staffers from a certifying company accredited by the U.S. Department of Agriculture. Organic and nonorganic products must not be manufactured at the same time, and equipment must be flushed out and sanitized before an organic production run. Paperwork must be verified and pest-control methods scrutinized, and the tea plantations must send a copy of their certification with every shipment of tea they export.

Getting to the point of Honest Tea being completely organic was like waiting for water to boil. Cost was not a problem: Though a ton of the best organic tea costs $5,000, significantly more than conventionally grown tea, it goes such a long way that the tea in a sixteen-ounce bottle still costs only about four cents. But while availability and consistent quality of the tea supply were iffy at first, Seth was more worried about tinkering with flavors that Honest Tea customers had grown to like. The most popular flavor, Moroccan Mint, had been made with green tea and refined mint oils, which Seth had to replace with organic peppermint and spearmint leaves and organic tea from a new source. To his relief and surprise, he explained, "The flavor actually improved"—and he was even more surprised when the total cost declined. (That didn't surprise me, by the way. Time and again, I have seen that it's actually less costly to use organic ingredients and green methods than it is to be conventionally "cost-efficient.") Even better, sales of Moroccan Mint chalked up double-digit gains after the switch.

Not everything went as well. USDA rules on organic production banned the use of malic acid, a stabilizer that kills bacteria, and substituting citric acid meant that Seth had to tweak his flavors to tone down the tartness. When a Mexican supplier's crop of agave cactus failed, Honest Tea had to do without that intense sweetener and use organic sugar until the cactus recovered. And an unsweetened flavor called Haarlem Honeybush, using an organic herb grown by a subsistence farming community in South Africa, proved too far-out for the market and had to be scrubbed. "It was too much about the mission and not enough about what our customers wanted," Seth admitted.

Nevertheless, Honest Tea stuck to its principles. Some of the revenues from Haarlem Honeybush went to the South Africans, just as proceeds from First Nation Peppermint were shared with the Native Americans who grew the mint. And in an interesting postscript to this story, Seth told me that the company's new sweetened tea called Pomegranate Red uses honeybush as an ingredient. So even though the community's name isn't on the label, Honest Tea may still be able to give it an economic boost.

Seth has always made sure that his regular suppliers can make a living by doing business with him—even if he has to pay them above-market prices for their crops. That's not softheaded, according to him (and me); it's a way of making sure no one cuts corners on quality.

It's also a measure of how deeply the notion of authenticity and integrity is embedded in Honest Tea's operations. The company delivers what it promises. That may sound simple, but it's rare in business today. And, as Seth and Barry discovered in their early focus groups, consumers have come to distrust the advertising hype spewed out by traditional beverage purveyors. They are fed up with claims that a 120-calorie beverage made of high-fructose corn syrup diluted with water is refreshing, great-tasting, and good for you. They feel betrayed and disrespected.

Honest Tea responds to this discontent with candor inside its bottles and out—one of the key tenets of the organic philosophy. An early test of the brand's organic honesty came when the company was preparing to market a flavor called Zero to underscore the fact that it packed no calories at all. The labels were already being printed when it was discovered that the sweetener, a fermented cane sugar, would actually add 3.5 calories per bottle. Playing by federal regulations, the drink could still be called Zero: Anything less than five calories can be passed off as zero in advertising and labeling. But Seth and Barry balked. Honest Tea meant honesty, and they wouldn't fudge. Instead, they added a bit more sweetening—agave this time, enough to bring the calorie count to ten. Then they called it Ten. As the chatty message on the back of the bottle boasts, "We started with the anti-oxidant power of green tea, an essence of tangerine, a touch of organic agave, and a revolutionary cane sugar . . . a hint of sweetness with nothing artificial and only 10 calories per bottle. Eureka! This drink is a perfect 10."

As befits a socially responsible organic enterprise, Honest Tea is on the lookout for ways it can help heal the environment. For one thing, it has introduced juice pouches that are reusable. In places that don't recycle the pouches, kids are encouraged to send them to the company in exchange for a seedling tree or to raise money for a favorite charity. In addition, the company has a partnership with Ford Motor Company in which Honest Tea–branded Escape hybrid vehicles tour the United States to raise awareness about sustainability.

In its own manufacturing operations, Honest Tea is working on a plan to turn spent tea leaves into organic plant fertilizer. As one might expect from a man who expressed his initial vision for the company in terms of tree planting, Seth is particularly keen on the notion of returning the company's organic ingredients back to the Earth.

The way Seth sees it, the company's sustainability efforts hinge on growth and balance. "We need to do the right thing," he says, but the company can't lose sight of its bottom line. If costs force it to raise its price so much that it can't compete and grow, then how can it do anything good for its consumers, its supplier communities, and the planet? "We have to be market savvy and business savvy in the way we approach our responsibilities," he points out. What else would you expect from a man whose watchwords are honesty and authenticity?

The experiences of the people showcased in this chapter tell me that organic is, quite simply, the best way to do business. Not just for Seth and Barry at Honest Tea or for me. It's true for anyone who wants to run a truly cost-efficient business—the only kind that can survive long-term—and still leave behind a habitable planet for our children. And as the next chapter makes unmistakably clear, the planet won't be habitable unless we all find ways to clean up the messes that conventional business leaves in its wake, never even counting the cost.

6

No Such Place as Away

My grandfather was the hardworking son of Eastern European immigrants, the sort of entrepreneur who built America's industrial base in the middle of the last century. He and my father owned and ran a shoe factory in Pittsfield, New Hampshire, called the Pittsfield Shoe Corporation, and it was located on the banks of the Suncook River. The factory employed a lot of people, it produced a good product line—and it was a polluter.

But I knew nothing of that. When I was young, I loved to watch the colored water—one minute red, another yellow, still another green—gushing out of the factory into the river. To me, the wastewater was beautiful. Only later did I learn that the Merrimack, into which our little river emptied and whose banks were crowded with shoe factories, was the tenth most polluted river in the United States. I had to face the fact that our family business, of which we were so proud, was a part of the problem.

The shoe business was slow to seek a solution. Part of the reason was cut-rate foreign competition—how could an embattled industry stay afloat if it was being forced to spend hundreds of thousands or even millions of dollars to reduce its impact on the environment? But that attitude, understandable if short-sighted, explained only a portion of the industry's inertia. The rest traced to the sheer disbelief of the shoe business's leaders. How could a little wastewater, they wondered, be worth such a fuss?

In those days, you understand, America felt so huge, and its distances seemed so expansive, that people believed their garbage somehow melted into the landscape and disappeared—that it simply went "away." You could throw it "away," flush it "away," and if you had a tailpipe or a smokestack, even blow it "away."

It sounds odd from today's perspective. It's as if "away" were some mythical, Oz-like place where all waste, trash, and associated ugliness could be disposed of without consequence. And we threw stuff away until it was piled higher than the fence around it, or killed the fish, or put a haze on the horizon.

It has taken us a shamefully long while, but at last we have learned that there is no such place as "away." The fact is, the planet Earth is a closed system. Whenever and wherever a light switch is thrown, a puff of smoke or some type of pollution is created where the power is generated. We may not see it, but it's there. My trash washes up on someone else's shore—or fouls their groundwater—just as surely as distant air pollution follows prevailing winds to my valley.

Think how far we've come, yet how far we have to go: Today, we find it laughable that anyone ever believed the world was flat. We marvel that it took Christopher Columbus's voyage of discovery in 1492 to disprove it once and for all. What's it going to take for the last stubborn few to accept that the idea of "away" is a myth worthy only of flat-earthers? We've already seen medical waste washing up on beaches, even after it's been taken miles out to sea. We've long seen birds struggle to free themselves from plastic six-pack rings stuck around their necks. It's simply delusional to think there is—or ever was—such a place as "away."

Every day, in everything we do, we are having an impact on the planet. If it's true for individuals, and it is, then it is certainly true for businesses. Any business owner or leader who doesn't see this is willfully blind, but that's not all. He or she is turning down the largest and most lucrative opportunity of this young century, which is to reduce or eliminate industrial waste. The companies that figure out how to do business with little or no waste are going to reduce their costs, boost their profits, and win tremendous public support as they do it. I fully intend for Stonyfield Farm to continue leading in this pursuit, and I want your company to be my competition.

There are people out there who excel in designing waste out of (and, I might add, profits into) a system—more and more of them every day. But if you're looking for real creativity and efficiency, you don't necessarily have to retain a consultant. You can learn a lot simply by paying attention to how nature handles waste. In nature, there is no waste—period. Every by-product of every process fuels or catalyzes some other process. Decomposed leaves feed mushrooms and fertilize wildflowers. Tiny insects feed on fungi that would otherwise overwhelm a tree. Old beaver dams provide spawning zones for fish. It's just amazing how efficient nature is, once you start paying attention to it.

As businesspeople, we need to strive to be just as efficient in handling waste as nature is. Ideally, each company and each process should be able to boast that everything that doesn't go out to the consumer goes back to the Earth. Any system that delivers less than total efficiency should be regarded as broken.

That last sentence sets up a high hurdle. But it also represents a very hopeful goal. What it says to us is, waste is inevitable—but dealing with it need not be an insurmountable obstacle to processes or products. If nature handles it, somehow we can, too.

Let me stop here for a moment and assure you that my strategies for reducing or eliminating waste did not spring fully formed from my subconscious. It's been a long evolution for me, as I'm sure it is for many. My goal is to shorten your evolutionary time line a bit, by sharing what I've learned.

In our early years at Stonyfield, we sometimes, and always reluctantly, dealt with waste by dumping it, much as my father and grandfather did, in the nearest version of "away." But it really bothered me. Having waste to dispose of always seemed, well, a waste.

If I needed an epiphany to make me truly serious about the problem, it came one snowy night when the dumpster outside the Yogurt Works caught fire. We were still on the farm, with Samuel's house and mine both connected to the barn, where all our cups and lids were stored, as well as the Yogurt Works and the office. We had supported our local recycling center back then, but it didn't take plastic, so we had a dumpster outside the barn. It turned out later that an employee had thrown a cigarette butt in there.

We were having dinner when I noticed that it was light

outside—this in February, long after dark. We ran outside and there was the dumpster, about ten feet from the barn, with twenty-foot flames belching up, dancing back and forth in the hilltop wind. The dumpster itself was literally orange, glowing with heat. The paint on the barn was already blistering and cracking, and I was afraid the whole place would go up in flames.

There was a volunteer fire department, but we were at the very end of the end of town and it was going to take them forever to arrive. I had no choice. I grabbed a chain, jumped onto the tractor, and backed up to the dumpster. My hair and skin were getting singed as I crawled through the snow to hook up the dumpster and drag it away from the barn to burn itself out in the driveway.

The next morning, the contents of the dumpster had cooled into one giant meteorite of plastic. We made two firm decisions that day. One was that nobody would ever smoke again anywhere on our hill. And the other was that, somehow, all our film and plastic would be recycled from that point on. We had to find a place to do it.

There was another, less dramatic turning point for Stonyfield's waste processing, and it came about twenty years ago when circumstances forced us to discard 3,600 plastic cups of unsellable runny yogurt. Incubator problems had kept the batch from reaching the right consistency, and we hadn't noticed the problem until it was neatly packaged and ready for shipping. I knew that I couldn't just put the load in a landfill, so we piled it on ten pallets, trucked it to a nearby pig farm, and began laboriously opening each cup. We intended to pour the contents into the pigs' trough and then rinse the cups for recycling.

I'll never forget the look on the farmer's face when he figured out what we were going to do. "Forget it," he said. "Just push those pallets off the truck, and watch what happens." As the cups rolled all over the ground, the farmer opened a gate and the pigs stampeded through. In a matter of seconds, they tore the cups apart and slurped up every ounce of yogurt, drooling, oinking, and stinking with a ferocity that left only a pile of plastic shreds licked absolutely clean. All we had to do was scoop up the debris with snow shovels and drive it to the local recycling center.

Thus did a herd of hungry pigs show me the way, back in 1986. I am forever grateful. Besides saving us the cost and trouble of washing out 3,600 yogurt cups, those pigs showed us—vividly—how little we knew about managing our waste in more efficient ways. Watching those pigs eat was a master seminar in how to slash costs and drive profits—without the consulting fee, the boxed lunch, or the stuffy conference room.

Since those porkers schooled me, however, I've learned that not everything works as perfectly as feeding cups of yogurt to pigs. It's largely unrealistic to think that we can avoid generating at least *some* waste. People are not going to lie down beneath a cow, mouths open wide, to get their dairy. We have to package it, and reducing the environmental impact of packaging is the Holy Grail of waste management—the goal everyone in industry is straining to meet.

It would be nice if there were a national strategy in place to guide companies seeking to do the right thing. Unfortunately, in the area of packaging waste, all we have is a crazy quilt of state initiatives begun under the 1976 Solid Waste Disposal Act. Huge landfills here, incinerators there. Curbside recycling programs in some communities, virtuous individuals left to scout out recyclers on their own in others. Worse yet, very little attention is given to the notion of stopping waste, say, by finding another use for an item or repairing something that's broken.

No wonder many businesspeople feel isolated and uncertain as to how to proceed. Lacking a coherent waste-management policy in this country, each company struggles to find a path for itself—or, too often, gives up entirely.

The Stonyfield Way with Waste

How have we wrestled with environmental stewardship at Stonyfield? With determination, I would say, tempered with a commitment to incremental improvement. I knew from the beginning that this wouldn't be an overnight proposition. I assumed we would learn a little bit more each year, and that technology and environmental knowledge would grow with us.

I also assumed that packaging should cease to be merely the province of marketers, and that waste management should be a company-wide concern. To that end, we have established a multidisciplinary team that has several key goals. The first and most important—the one that supersedes all others—is to ensure that Stonyfield Farm's packaging is 100 percent sustainable by the year 2015. That's a huge feat to accomplish, but it's an endeavor that our employees have wholeheartedly embraced. They have dug into the research, challenging all assumptions (especially mine), and they have stepped up whenever extra effort was required.

One of the first and most important data points we collected, the one that spurred us on our way back in the early 1990s, was found in a study conducted by Boston's Tellus Institute. The researchers weighed a range of packaging options, from plastics and the poly-coated paper used in milk cartons to glass and metals. The surprising upshot was that package *production,* not disposal, was the leading environmental villain.

Over more than twenty years, that fact has not changed. Would you believe that less than 5 percent of the environmental impact of packaging is to be found in the final disposal stage? More than 95 percent of the ecological damage comes from the energy used and the toxins created in the package-manufacturing and delivery process. The conclusion is as true today as it was when the study was first done: Except for highly toxic materials like PVC, the lightest package is the best package for the environment.

We decided to start making our yogurt cups out of polypropylene, the lightest-weight but still durable plastic for preformed cups. The drawback was that injection-molded polypropylene plastic was and is still not recyclable in most communities. Even so, we use so much less plastic to make our yogurt cups—17 percent less, in fact—that, compared to alternative materials, the polypropylene ended up being the better environmental choice. For instance, we now prevent the manufacture and disposal of nearly 200 tons less plastic than we would if we used the more widely recyclable HDPE (#2) plastic. In addition, our decision preserved nonrenewable resources (it takes oil to make plastic) and kept tons of atmospheric emissions from the manufacture and distribution of the packaging out of the air. This was all good, and we were proud of ourselves. But not for a moment did we believe that polypropylene was the end-state solution for us. We only knew that it would have to do until something better came along.

Part of the answer came along soon, in the form of the lid. In 2002, guided by a University of Michigan Center for Sustainable Systems study of our packaging, we eliminated plastic lids and inner seals in favor of foil and, in so doing, saved more than $1 million per year. The switch reduced solid waste by 6 percent annually and cut back on the amount of energy (16 percent) and water (13 percent) needed to turn out a cup of yogurt.

Still, aluminum foil feels like just another step along our road to sustainable manufacturing. We aren't resting on our laurels. We're continuing to move forward, and setting annual goals for incremental improvement.

Between 2007 and 2015, when we expect to reach our 100 percent sustainability goal, we have made a commitment to achieve at least 10 percent annual improvement in sustainable packaging.

So, like a fisherman seeking to improve the chances of hauling in his limit, we throw the nets far and wide in search of elusive prey—the fully sustainable packaging method that will wring another few percentage points out of our goal. Recently, for example, Stonyfield has considered developing yogurt containers made from crops such as beets, corn, and potatoes.

A plasticlike material from vegetables? It sounds strange, I know, but chances are you've already eaten a takeout meal using a fork made from corn, especially if the restaurants you frequent have environmental sustainability as a goal. Why not use the same recipe, or something similar, to make yogurt containers? Biopolymers—plastics made from agricultural products like corn—are becoming more commonly available. And they pose enormous potential for the future. However, using corn as an example, it is not the panacea it may appear. That's because the growing of corn sucks up inputs (water, fuel, pesticides, and energy-intensive fertilizer). The true potential of biopolymers will come when we can make them from the waste from farming and processing of food—not from virgin crops.

If our investigations into innovative container materials bear fruit, your cup of Stonyfield yogurt might someday look and feel the same as today's plastic version, but the container itself will add nutrition to the yogurt it holds. Furthermore, it won't require disposal. No more stuffing your empty cup into an already choked trash or recycling bin; you might instead choose to eat it as a second course, or toss it onto your compost pile, returning it to its carbon roots.

Warming to the challenge of using as little plastic and cardboard as possible, we've swapped injection-molded, preformed cups for ones that are actually made by the machine that also fills them with yogurt. In what's known as a "form, fill, and seal" packaging process, the cups are stamped from gigantic rolls of plastic film, leaving hardly any scrap behind. The finished package weighs 37 percent less than injection-molded cups.

Some of the packaging changes we've made originated from a 1999 assessment by the University of Michigan's Center for Sustainable Systems, which looked at Stonyfield Farm's entire product-delivery system (PDS)—from the manufacturing of the materials used in our packaging through to the consumer. Everything was on the table—from our yogurt cup's inner seal and its multipack outer wrap, to the corrugated boxes and pallets used in shipping and the various transportation links that bring the materials to us and take the yogurt to our customers.

Interestingly, the study showed that the size of our containers had a much bigger impact on the environment than did either the materials themselves or the process used to make them. It takes 27 percent less energy per pound of yogurt to produce and distribute our yogurt in thirty-two-ounce containers than it does to turn out six-ounce cups. If we sold only the quart-size containers, we could save about 25,000 barrels of oil a year, adding nearly $1 million to our bottom line. But our consumers would have to be on board with the one-size-fits-all idea, and even I have to admit that thirty-two ounces of our yogurt is way too much for a brown-bag lunch. What works best for the customer has to be our guide—always.

That was an unfortunate but inescapable lesson: Not every environmentally good idea is a sound business idea as well. But that doesn't stop us from forging ahead with innovative concepts. Sometimes we overreach our grasp or run into roadblocks, but one thing is certain: It's an education every step of the way.

Consider Stonyfield Farm's liquid and solid waste issues, because we have those to contend with, too.

When I talk about liquid waste, I'm talking about the water we use to rinse the equipment when we change from one product line or flavor to another. This rinse water contains milk, yogurt, fruit, and flavorings—nothing bad, but nothing that belongs in water, either.

Our solid waste consists mainly of cupped yogurt from a variety of sources, including samples from our quality control process. While we try to minimize the waste we generate, we are still far from zero waste.

Where the yogurt waste was concerned, our first thought was of the pigs that had done such a snortin' good job for us decades ago. We paid to install a feed tank at a New Hampshire pig farm, and the farmer even branded his pork to local restaurants for a while as "Stonyfield Farm yogurt–fed." But our production soon grew beyond the pigs' abilities to pig out. Since so many farms have disappeared in New Hampshire, there are simply not enough pig farmers to take our yogurt. Just getting the solid waste off our site took fifty-two tractor-trailers hauling 2.5 million pounds of trash per year.

Meanwhile, doors were closing on the liquid-waste side, too. There came a point when the town of Londonderry told us they couldn't continue to accept our rinse water. Londonderry leases its wastewater capacity from nearby Manchester, where the regional sewage treatment plant is located. Thanks to residential and commercial growth in and around Londonderry, the city maxed out its treatment allocation and sent us packing. It was strictly a matter of capacity. We'd gotten too big for the system.

Our answer to both the liquid- and the solid-waste problems was to build our own ecological pretreatment plant. Since the spring of 2006, we've been turning waste yogurt into methane gas and using it as part of the energy we consume. Believe me when I tell you that building a pretreatment plant hadn't been high on our list of priorities. The project required huge amounts of capital, money we could have used to make more yogurt and expand into new markets. But when the town was forced to limit our liquid-waste discharges, we saw an opportunity for a great leap forward that would make Stonyfield more environmentally sound.

That's not to say we didn't look hard before we leaped. Indeed, we had two very big problems to solve first. The first was technical, the second more corporate in nature—but related to the technical issue, too.

Aerobic biological systems are the standard in the dairy industry. These systems use bacteria and oxygen to "eat" waste material, leaving the water clean enough to put back into a river. But that model requires a great deal of energy and would leave us with large amounts of sludge that would have to be hauled to that mythical place called "away." We didn't want to become a net hauler of a different type of waste, even if it was mostly organic. So we opted to use bacteria but in an oxygen-free, or anaerobic, system known as a digester. The methane by-product could be used as fuel to heat the system, and the amount of sludge left behind would be greatly reduced.

Our second problem concerned our partner, Groupe Danone. Our agreement with them required me to get approval for any capital spending of more than $1 million. Initially, the people at Danone said no to the pretreatment facility, having had a bad experience with an anaerobic system that failed. But after I showed them the innovative designs of our supplier, ADI Systems in New Brunswick, Canada, and convinced them that the technology was much improved, the Danone people went along with our plan.

The payoff has been enormous. The new system cost 15 percent more to build than an aerobic plant, but it uses 40 percent less energy and generates 90 percent less waste. Instead of the treatment system resulting in one to two trucks of sludge per week, as had been projected for the standard aerobic approach, we now have been operating for more than a year without hauling any sludge at all and expect to produce just a few truckloads every three years. With a 50 percent reduction in operating costs, and projected savings of $3.6 million over the system's first ten years, the extra capital investment will pay for itself very quickly.

We are now in the process of designing a separating operation that removes yogurt generated or rejected by our quality control process from its cup and separates the aluminum-foil lid from its seal, eliminating the need to truck the material a good distance away just to get the job done. Better yet, the waste yogurt can be mixed with rinse water and pumped as slurry for the short distance to our digester, saving still more trucking.

Our sustainable packaging team is looking at more than material. Each year we try to understand a bit more about our packaging, in the belief that the more we know, the more we can improve. This year the team, under our vice president of purchasing, Rolf Carlson, is focusing on creating a sustainability scorecard for the materials themselves, but also for the manufacturing process. By devoting resources to these initiatives, we hope to pave the way for continuing improvements and reductions.

And if anyone can find a way to reduce waste, it will be Nancy and her team. I know no one more passionate on the subject. She tells a story about a recent trip to Ecuador, to visit our organic banana supplier there, and driving past fields of conventional bananas and sugarcane stretching for miles. At one point she saw some children happily splashing in a water hole, and she stopped, intending to take a photo of the charming scene. Then she realized—an "Oh, my God" moment, she said—that the water was runoff from the fields, loaded with who knows what pesticides and herbicides. She said it sent shivers down her spine to think what the stuff was doing to those kids and made her grateful that Stonyfield only buys organic bananas that will not put poisons into the local environment.

Reduce or Redesign, Reuse, Recycle—In That Order

I'm convinced that smart, hardworking people can profit from practicing what many people call the R's of effective waste management. The R's aren't new, but the order of priority is much more important than people realize. Specifically:

- *Reduce or redesign* (or both) by using less material and resources and producing less waste. This is where you get the biggest net environmental impact—and net profit.
- *Reuse* by putting used materials and products back into service. This is the second biggest waste-saving and money-saving opportunity, much larger than through recycling.
- *Recycle* by transforming used materials and products into new ones. Recycling is the buzzword that gets people's attention, but it really is the lowest-priority choice and the slowest payback option.

At Stonyfield, we've learned that reducing waste means consuming less and discarding less. And since source reduction, particularly when it comes to packaging, stops waste before it starts, it's the most economical and ecological choice.

Incorporating reusable materials and equipment into a production operation like ours is difficult but not impossible. For example, the fruit that goes into Stonyfield yogurt used to come to us in throwaway plastic bags inside cardboard boxes. We plugged that leak by replacing the bags with five-gallon plastic buckets, which were reused by manufacturers of wallboard paste. However, too many were still winding up in landfills, so we plugged that leak, too. Now most of our fruit preparations arrive in big, stainless-steel totes that resemble oversize beer kegs. The totes can be washed and used over and over again. It's less expensive and easier for us not to have to handle mountains of empty fruit bags or buckets, and it's easier on the environment. Another example of reuse is with the cardboard boxes that our plastic cups are shipped in. Over a decade ago we found a company that buys them from us—and resells them to clothing and auto parts manufacturers to ship their products. Hopefully the boxes will be used many times before they are recycled.

Recycling is almost universally regarded as a virtue. I beg to differ. The act of recycling actually means that we have failed to reduce or reuse. The EPA's own numbers delineate that failure: Each of us now produces 4.4 pounds of waste each day, nearly twice as much as thirty-five years ago. Consequently, we have to spend enormous amounts of energy and money carting away all of this waste to someplace else, where it will be made into something different—a process that releases still more CO_2 into the atmosphere.

What is more, recycling affects only a fraction of solid waste. At best, 5 percent of plastic gets recycled. We do better with aluminum cans, but the recycle rate is still only 30 to 35 percent.

Even when commonly used and supposedly recyclable waste materials are taken to a recycling center, the energy contained in them isn't necessarily recaptured. Take certain yogurt cups and soft-drink bottles made of polyethylene. Look on their bottoms and you're likely to see the number 2, meaning they are made of the same base resin. Yet your municipal recycling plant likely accepts only the bottles. This is because all number 2 plastics are not the same. The number 2 used to make bottles has a different melting point than that used to make wide-mouth containers like yogurt cups. Since they are different, they cannot generally be recycled together. Little surprise, then, that so many supposedly recyclable plastic containers end up in landfills.

At Stonyfield, we still recycle, but only as a last resort after we've tried to design waste out of the product or process. We've been working for many years with a Waltham, Massachusetts–based company, Recycline, that makes toothbrush and razor handles from our used cups.

As part of its quest to become a green giant, Wal-Mart has pledged to eliminate a quarter of the solid waste currently produced by its U.S. facilities. When the company took an environmental impact team up on its suggestion that Wal-Mart bundle for resale the plastic that it used to send to landfills or incinerators, the company saved $28 million a year. Another

$2.4 million of cost savings was lopped off by asking the supplier of its private-label Kid Connection line of toys to eliminate unneeded packaging. Wal-Mart now ships nearly five hundred fewer containers each year, reducing shipping costs and saving 3,800 trees and a million barrels of oil in the bargain.

Indeed, here's how CEO Lee Scott wants his employees to think about waste: "If we throw it away, we had to buy it first. So we pay twice—once to get it, once to have it taken away. What if we reverse that? What if our suppliers send us less, and everything they send us has value as a recycled product? No waste, and we get paid instead." Smart talk.

And speaking of smart talk, when it comes to seizing waste-based opportunities that boost a company's bottom line, the grand master is my friend Ray Anderson, founder and chairman of Atlanta-based Interface. In his quest to erase Interface's environmental footprint while boosting its profits, nothing escapes Ray's attention.

Interface Sweeps Waste Out from Under Its Rug

The carpet industry casts a huge shadow in Georgia. More than forty-five thousand people work in the state's carpet mills, earning wages of some $4 billion a year in a business that accounts for $10 billion of the state's overall economic activity. But thanks to forward-looking industry leaders like Ray, whom I've known for more than ten years, the carpet industry is leaving an environmental footprint far less visible and damaging than one might ever imagine. "Reduce or redesign; reuse; recycle" is not just the Interface gospel; it's the message Ray is fervently spreading throughout the carpet and flooring industry—indeed, throughout business as a whole.

He has been enormously successful as the head of a $1 billion company that leads the world in the design and production of so-called carpet tiles, the modular squares that can be laid down and taken up easily, just the thing for a wired world in which access to under-floor connections is such a cost-effective feature of office space. Interface, which also makes broadloom carpet and (until its recent divestiture) commercial fabrics, does business in more than one hundred countries and has manufacturing plants on four continents.

Despite his tailored suits, Ray isn't your typical captain of industry. He makes clear in his Georgia drawl that he'd rather be known as, say, "a radical industrialist," than as a conventional carpet mogul. Commercial carpet making, after all, has long been a highly toxic business. It has depended on petroleum products for its synthetic fibers and on problematic glass fiber and polyvinyl chloride for its carpet backings, spewing out greenhouse gases and toxin-laden water as manufacturing waste by-products. Moreover, worn-out carpets end up as virtually indestructible components of garbage mountains and underground waste pits.

With that legacy behind him, it's no wonder that when Ray makes his case for planetary sustainability as unparalleled profit opportunity, he sounds like a repentant sinner, compelled to atone and eager to share the good news of salvation. He names his own sins as plundering the Earth, polluting the environment, and stealing resources that belonged not to him but to future generations. He's determined to make up for past transgressions by completely erasing his business's environmental footprint and by bringing others into the sustainability fold. Reducing waste and reshaping what remains into reusable raw material is a big part of Ray's vision.

Ray underwent his eco-conversion in 1994, when he realized the extent of industry's destructiveness and vowed to become a new kind of businessman, one who puts back into the environment everything he takes out. For the previous twenty years, this smart and ambitious Georgia Tech–educated engineer had been immersed in making a success of Interface, which he founded in 1973. But in 1994, he was asked by ecology-minded interior designers what Interface was doing to help the Earth. He looked blankly. "Nothing" about covered it, and the question stayed with him.

Seeking to educate himself, Ray found a book that changed his life—Paul Hawken's *The Ecology of Commerce.* Reading Hawken's account of species extinction, of the fouling of air and water, and of "the death of birth," a phrase that particularly stunned Ray, was like taking "a spear to the chest," he recalls. He responded by vowing to make his company totally sustainable by 2020, meaning that it will produce no toxic waste or dangerous emissions and will use no oil whatsoever. Ray says Interface is over 40 percent of the way to that goal.

What Ray preaches to anyone who will listen is not fire and brimstone, but the chance for acolytes to earn redemption and greater profits all at the same time—hardly a penance for any company thinking of following his lead. He points to the $336 million of savings Interface has enjoyed in little more than a decade just from its waste-reduction efforts alone. He regales listeners with tales of hard times weathered and new business won, thanks to technological advances and design innovations inspired by the company's environmental initiatives. Who can argue with an ecological message built on lower costs, better products and processes, motivated employees, and an admirable image? And Ray has the numbers to back up his claims: Over the three years ending January 1, 2007, Interface's annual gross profit rose more than 52 percent to $339.6 million. Operating income surged 130 percent to $72 million while its share price has gone from $6 to $20.

Ray and I agree that efficient waste reduction is a two-part process: First, reduce the input of raw materials, particularly the nonrenewable kind. Second, reduce the output of byproducts that nature cannot absorb nor industry reuse and that end up harming the environment. Accordingly, Interface defines waste as "any cost that does not provide value" to its customers—in effect, it is the product of inefficiency, of not doing something "right the first time." So, besides its effort to eliminate flawed goods and scraps that end up clogging landfills, the company works hard to use as little as possible of any material and to stem losses caused by shipping errors and mistakes on invoices. That means that both products and processes are being redesigned with an eye to generating only the kind of waste that can be turned into a resource—or a "technical nutrient," as Interface styles it—for another product.

The gist of Interface's waste policy can be summarized with one word: Simplify. The corporate acronym for it is anything but simple: QUEST (Quality Utilizing Employee Suggestions and Teamwork). Fortunately, the policy itself is crystal clear—using fewer resources is always better than recycling or reclaiming.

At Interface's plant in Guilford, Maine, for example, managers cut water usage by 65 percent, saving more than 2 million gallons a year. How did the Guilford crew do it? With a few minor adjustments to a heat- and water-recovery system and the installation of a brass nozzle that changed the water flow pattern. The nozzle cost Interface $8.50; the savings add up to $10,000 a year. Not a bad return on investment, and proof of the fact that getting rid of waste need not be a long and costly business.

Another manager at the Guilford plant decided that too much antistatic agent was being used in the dyeing operation, which led him to check out an alternative product. The result was a money-saving, environmentally friendly reduction of 83 percent in antistatic chemical use. That achievement sparked further dyeing-process evaluations that did away with acetic acid altogether in favor of a more benign alternative.

Interface's catalog of waste-reduction gains also shows lighter but more durable carpet tile products, with as much as a pound less material per square yard, and a modular-carpet-making process that uses an astonishing 81 percent less water than it did in 1996. In addition, the company's energy use at its carpet manufacturing facilities has declined by 45 percent, and the manufacturing waste Interface carts off to landfills has shrunk by 70 percent, from more than 20 million pounds in 1996 to around 7.5 million in 2006.

But there's more to Interface's solid-waste-reduction program than simply cutting back on trash. It strives to turn manufacturing leftovers and previously used materials into valuable raw material for another product cycle, which reduces material purchases and costs, eases the strain on the Earth's natural resources, and lessens the amount of waste that goes into landfills. This manufacturing trifecta, in turn, frees up capital that can be invested in sustainable technologies and saves consumers money by providing them with less-expensive products.

Among the company's innovations are nylon yarn made from reclaimed carpet face pile (part of its ReEntry carpet-reclamation program), backing material made from waste goods and previously used carpet backing, and new textiles woven from fibers reclaimed from polyester fabric. Innovations making their way through the pipeline also include raw materials made from plants such as hemp, sugarcane, and corn.

Ray Anderson believes—and I agree—that we are in the early days of a new industrial revolution, one driven by gentler techniques and technologies that mimic nature's ways. And as a former debaser of the environment, he is grateful for the chance to help renew and sustain the Earth, while reorienting his company and the world at large toward "a new and better way to bigger profits and to greater, more genuine shareholder value." A combination of conviction and success makes Ray Anderson a very persuasive voice for the notion that a business can manufacture without waste and grow without damaging the environment.

Terracycle, Inc.—Worming Its Way to Success

Mother Nature's got nothing on Tom Szaky—well, not much, anyway. There is no waste in her world, and there's precious little in Tom's, either. Tom understands that what most of us consider to be waste is nothing more than raw material for production.

Tom Szaky is the cofounder of TerraCycle, a Trenton, New Jersey, start-up whose flagship product is liquid plant fertilizer. But it's not *what* he does that warrants the comparison with natural systems; it's *how* he does it. Tom's fast-growing company uses waste to make waste. He then packages it in bottles made from waste and sells the product to a growing legion of satisfied customers who like it enough to, well, not waste it.

Let's break it down some more. What Tom and TerraCycle do is take organic waste—composted vegetables, for example—and feed it to a quarter million worms that eat their body weight in landfill-bound trash every day. Then TerraCycle collects the worm poop—that's the indelicate word the company prefers—and sells it in a liquefied form quaintly known as "tea." Even the packaging is derived from waste material—namely used twenty-ounce soda bottles they collect from schoolchildren, among other donors. (They pay a nickel a bottle as a fund-raising contribution.) All Szaky and company do is wash those bottles and remove the labels. Then they put on a label of their own, screw on a spray top they've gotten as surplus from another manufacturer, and load the finished product into someone else's misprinted shipping boxes. Before sending them out into the gardening world, TerraCycle takes care to ensure that every box of bottles has a variety of colors and shapes, just to reinforce the recycled nature of the packaging.

TerraCycle began its young life as an entry in a university business-plan competition in 2001. Szaky and a fellow freshman Princeton University student named Jon Beyer wanted to prove that a business could be run with a nearly negative cost structure, and to them, selling worm poop sounded like the way to put the theory to the test. They had a friend who grew plants of a particular species in his basement, and they had seen what repeated applications of worm poop could do for that guy's production, so they thought why not try to commercialize the idea? When it came time to write the plan, it certainly didn't hurt that Beyer's father was an ecotoxicologist who knew plenty about worms. Szaky and Beyer came in fourth, which was great, but that wasn't good enough to win a cash prize.

They won the next contest they entered, however, and received a check for $200. Then they entered another low-stakes contest and won that, too. And then another, and another. All told, they entered seven business-plan competitions, capped by Carrot Capital's very prestigious contest, which offered a $1 million purse. Much to their shock, they won that one, too. But they turned down the payday—and walked away knowing they had only $500 in the bank to come home to. Turns out Carrot Capital, a New York–based venture capital group, wanted to let everyone go except Tom, making him something akin to a spokesman for what would become their fertilizer. Tom wasn't interested. He rather liked the idea of running his own company, surrounded by people who shared a passion for literally pulling profit from trash cans.

So Tom went his own way, leaving school to devote his full energy to TerraCycle. Beyer stayed in school and eventually graduated, but remained involved in the technological end of the company. Szaky's first significant move was to borrow money from everyone he knew and max out his credit cards to buy the "worm gin" that would be central to the TerraCycle process. It was essentially a series of conveyer belts stacked atop one another to bring garbage to the worms, and it was available from its Florida developer in prototype form at a price of $20,000. The money was raised, but just barely.

Then Szaky, with Beyer's help, amassed the necessary production vats and tanks for mixing the worm-poop potions. Each was recycled from some other purpose and found in a landfill—some were horse tanks, others were thousand-gallon storage tanks that had their tops cut off. Eventually a headquarters building was purchased in a tough neighborhood of Trenton and painted with graffiti by can-wielding locals who were invited to use the walls to showcase their work. Tom furnished the HQ with cast-off desks and computers, and put lots of college interns in front of them.

One of the competitive aces TerraCycle has always held is its ability to offer retailers higher-than-average margins, because TerraCycle's own margins are so high. The worms work for free, after all. Still, no one is quite sure how Szaky managed to talk the likes of Wal-Mart and Home Depot into carrying his products. Then as now, Szaky greets the world in rumpled jeans and a T-shirt. But I can bet how he carried the day during those crucial presentations. When Tom Szaky opens his mouth, he doesn't miss a cue or a beat. He may have started his company as a nineteen-year-old college dropout, but he has matured into the role of a most persuasive twenty-four-year-old eco-entrepreneur.

From today's perspective, TerraCycle seems to have done everything right thus far. It was Szaky who realized that all soda bottles take the same size cap, meaning that these recyclable bottles were the ideal and most available source of cost-free packaging. He was also smart to seek and obtain organic certification for his plant food, because it lent the company instant credibility with gardeners. Certainly it didn't hurt in those early days when *The New York Times* called TerraCycle's plant food "the most eco-friendly product ever made." With that endorsement, plus literally dozens of high-visibility free-media opportunities each year, the transformation to hot-company status has long been complete. TerraCycle crossed the $5 million revenue threshold in 2007. The new waste-based TerraCycle products that are coming on line—including planting soil, seed-starter trays, and a deer repellent—are expected to generate a new spurt of growth to move the company toward $10 million in years to come—or to spur its public offering, whichever comes first.

None of this should suggest there haven't been glitches along the way: Szaky and Beyer found their first source of organic waste in the Princeton University dining halls, abundantly so, but they couldn't always get it to the worms before it became putrid. The two were forced to sort the reeking bags by the scoopful themselves because employees balked (or worse, became ill). Talk about hands-on. They almost quit the business before it got started.

Szaky also nearly got into trouble some years ago when he decided that the best way to find lots of soda bottles for packaging would be to gather them from curbside recycling bins throughout Trenton. Lo and behold, the practice turns out to be illegal. That's why schoolchildren are pocketing TerraCycle nickels today.

TerraCycle's latest hurdle is a lawsuit filed by Scott's, the lawn-and-garden behemoth that markets MiracleGro plant food. Scott's alleges that TerraCycle's packaging looks too much like theirs, both products having a circle on the label and some yellow (although TerraCycle's looks more goldenrod-toned, and no fewer than 120 other products on the market feature green-and-yellow labels).

Scott's and TerraCycle are also arguing about their respective research claims, but at last word, neither was allowing the other a look at the data. Szaky earned the ire of Scott's by publicizing a study conducted at the Rutgers University Eco-Complex that concluded that TerraCycle's liquid plant food performed as well or better than Miracle-Gro on most compared indices, and that unlike Miracle-Gro, TerraCycle can't be overapplied and cause plant burn. So far, Szaky and company are not cowering from the fight. They're emphasizing the David-and-Goliath nature of the dispute on their Web site and taking the issue public, encouraging customers to write to Scott's and tell them to back off. The message from TerraCycle to its customers is that Scott's is trying to prevent waste-based plant foods from succeeding in the marketplace, and must be stopped.

Beyond these inevitable consequences of doing well in business, Szaky faces only two significant challenges to fulfilling the business-from-garbage scheme he envisioned five years ago. The first is, will he ever actually achieve the negative cost stream he still thinks is possible? On the TerraCycle Web site, Szaky and company offer a long economic treatise on the theoretical feasibility of running a waste-based business with a negative cost structure. Still, Szaky has not yet found an economical way to get people to pay him to haul away the waste he feeds the worms, so that's kept him on the plus-side of the cost ledger. But he hasn't given up trying to drive the company toward the minus side.

Szaky's second problem looks smaller, but it may prove to be almost as tricky to solve as the first. It's the bottle caps—what to do with all those bottle caps that come into the factory with the soda bottles. Szaky and all his bright, creative employees are stumped. They've thrown it open to all comers now, through a contest on terracycle.net. Figure out what to do with all those bottle caps, and you win a lifetime free supply of—what else?—liquefied worm poop.

If you've come with me this far, you probably agree that the Earth needs more Ray Andersons and Tom Szakys—desperately and right away. It's fine and fitting to lament the oncoming decades of global warming and Katrina-like disasters, the disregard for nature that increasingly endangers all living creatures. But hand-wringing gets us nowhere; alarmists are only slightly more useful than polluters. The times cry out for pragmatists more than idealists; for hardheaded, profit-hungry entrepreneurs who see the looming crisis as an opportunity to be seized and leveraged like any other.

And any entrepreneur aiming to chase that goal could do a lot worse than model him- or herself and business on the family farmers who supply the bulk of our country's burgeoning organic crops. The next chapter looks at their methods and practices—and at their rewards, not least of which is their lifestyle.

7

Nurturing Those Who Nurture the Earth

By 1984, our herd had grown to nineteen cows. Every morning and evening, Samuel went next door and hooked up our brown-eyed Jersey cows to electric milking machines. They gave enough milk to produce 350 cases of yogurt a week.

Then one blustery winter night, high winds knocked out our power lines, leaving us in darkness. Samuel came into the office and told me that only one cow had been milked. By the dim light of two kerosene lanterns, Samuel, Louise, and I milked the cows by hand. But we were slow at the job, and the cows were unsettled by the change in routine; they kept kicking over the milk buckets. By the time we finished the last cow, it was nearly time to start over again. Never before had our careers seemed so ripe for change.

Sometime during the night, we decided to sell the cows. And before sunset the next day, the cows were gone, sold to two local farmers, Sheldon Sawyer and Bud and Betsy Booth. We still got the milk the girls produced, though, buying it from our friends. It was a pivotal moment for us as yogurt makers, both emotionally and commercially. We had finally gotten past the notion that using milk from cows other than our own would somehow compromise our product. And by switching from four-legged suppliers to the two-legged variety, we freed up much-needed time to think about other aspects of our business.

Down (Way Down) on the Farm

I have a special admiration for family farmers, their lifestyle, and their guiding values. I've come to see family farmers as the stewards of the earth under our feet. For most of us, they provide our most essential and important link to nature and the Earth's bounties. And, because they live on the land they steward, family farmers are generally more conscientious and conserving of their patch of the planet. As agricultural methods and farm finances go, so goes the health of the planet—and, by extension, the health of every one of us.

I grew up in the rapidly suburbanizing, but still partly rural outskirts of a New England city. Dotting the roads nearby were several dairy, poultry, and vegetable farms. But I gave them, along with the locally produced foods my family enjoyed, little thought—until they disappeared, swept away by a changing view of land use and an ebbing tide of farm profitability. The open fields, barns, and chicken coops of my childhood were replaced by housing developments and industrial parks.

I became brutally aware of the big changes in my New Hampshire landscape midway through high school. Kevin Cullen, a wonderful English teacher who had escaped the urban jungle for our rural hills, told me about Scott and Helen Nearing's classic books, *Living the Good Life* and *Continuing the Good Life,* which hailed the joys of self-reliance, being close to the land, and raising your own healthy food. I later became good friends with Helen, and we corresponded for years. I was intrigued by humanity's connection to nature, and began to sense—even if I couldn't quite explain it yet—that the loss of family farms would have a profound impact on both our country and our planet.

Later, when I came to know farmers who were struggling, I began to realize the complexity of the system and why those farms that were such a familiar part of my youth had disappeared. Simply put: Federal policies to cheapen our food supply worked so well that farmland became much more valuable as sites for houses, golf courses, and retail developments than it was for raising animals and growing crops. So, in 1973, for example, a nearby vegetable farmer I knew ran up against a summer drought with a new twist: The water table had been depleted by lawn-sprinkling neighbors in a big new development and country club nearby. The farmer couldn't pump enough water to save his crops, so he had no choice but to sell his farm and abandon his way of life. His story has been repeated many times over in the past few decades. And, tragically and needlessly, it is still happening today.

Take milk, for instance. Between 1989 and 2006, the price of conventionally produced milk went up and down with regularity, starting at $12.37 per "hundredweight" (about 12.4 cents per pound, or roughly a pint of milk) and ending below where it started, at $12.32 per hundredweight. The highest price reached over that seventeen-year span was $14.20 per hundredweight in 1998, with the lowest price, $10.57, registered just two years later. The rapidity of the decline was breathtaking and devastating for the dairy farmers caught in the avalanche: At 10.5 cents a pint, even the most efficient producer in America will lose money on milk.

As if rock-bottom prices weren't bad enough, there was no discernible pattern to the price fluctuations. They had nothing to do with supply and demand or weather patterns or phases of the moon. The price goes up and down based on an antiquated index of cheese prices in Wisconsin. And, incredibly, conventional dairy farmers have no idea how much they're earning for their work until the checks arrive in the mail a month after the cows have been milked and the milk has been sold.

What Went Wrong

Farm life has never been easy. It's a dawn-to-dusk proposition made even more daunting by floods and droughts, hail and high winds, killing frost and devastating diseases that can wipe out a year's or a lifetime's work in a matter of minutes. But U.S. government policies of the last three decades have done the most damage: The once ubiquitous and self-sustaining family farm has been sacrificed on the altar of multibillion-dollar agribusinesses.

The federal government, according to author Michael Pollan, got involved in farming as part of Franklin Roosevelt's New

Deal to help a Depression-battered economy. To smooth out the feast-and-famine cycles that were driving U.S. farmers into bankruptcy, Congress passed a series of laws mandating price supports and production controls. When prices of corn, wheat, rice, cotton, and such fell below production costs, farmers could hold their crops off a glutted market, using loans from the government to tide them over until prices recovered, at which point they could sell their stored crops and repay their government loans. They were also rewarded for letting land lie fallow to reduce surpluses and rejuvenate the soil. The ultimate goal was to raise disastrously low crop prices and thus make farming economically viable.

If prices stayed low for too long, farmers could repay their loans in kind, turning over stored grain to the government. The program cost the government little, since most of the loans were repaid in cash, and the surplus products could be sold when prices eventually rose, with the proceeds booked on the federal ledger. Sales from government agricultural stocks also helped to stabilize consumer product prices, keeping them from rising dramatically during droughts or natural disasters that cut into the harvest.

The system worked well, even though New Deal opponents and business interests, such as fertilizer and pesticide producers and grain speculators who stood to prosper from surplus crop production, searched long for ways to dismantle it. They found their opening in 1972, when 30 million tons of U.S. grain were sold to the Soviet Union, which had the effect of pushing up domestic grain prices to record highs. The price increase rippled through the system onto supermarket shelves, causing a consumer (read: voter) backlash. So, under the guise of fighting inflation, President Nixon's agriculture secretary,

Earl Butz, set about changing government policy to boost farm output and slash prices at the grocery store.

"Get big or get out" was the message to growers of the five largest crops—corn, cotton, rice, soybeans, and wheat. Agribusiness, not family farming, was the new and preferred model. And with commodity prices so high, Butz ran into little opposition to his plan to end Uncle Sam's role as a buyer of surplus crops. The New Deal system of loan-based price supports had helped to keep land idle when prices were low, and that had benefited the small farmer. Now Butz substituted direct payments to farmers. They would still be compensated when crop prices fell below a prescribed level—a constantly diminishing target, as it turned out—but there was no longer a floor under prices.

It didn't take long for the perversity of the new system to become clear. With no incentive to hold back crops or leave fields lying fallow, increasingly huge, factory-style producers could and did flood the market with grains and cotton. And why not? The government made no distinction between the family and the corporate farmer, funneling billions of dollars of crop subsidy payments into the pockets of some of the wealthiest people and corporations in the United States. Media mogul Ted Turner, for instance, and David Rockefeller, heir to a fabled fortune and a wealthy and successful banker in his own right, have each received hundreds of thousands of dollars in federal farm subsidies.

To get their government paychecks, these lucky "farmers" don't even have to get their hands dirty. All they have to do is invest in huge corporate farming operations that grow one of the favored big five crops, which account for more than 90 percent of all farm subsidies. Need or income levels are never considered. Some of the biggest winners are huge companies like John Hancock—which I've always associated with the insurance business, not farming—that happen to have a unit or subdivision with some sort of link to agriculture. Hancock raked in federal farm subsidies totaling $2.3 million in 2002 alone.

In fact, the bigger and wealthier the grower, the more government largesse it can expect to reap. Almost two-thirds of all farm subsidies paid out in 2005 went to only 10 percent of the recipient pool. As you might guess, when bigger is better, the small family farmer doesn't stand a chance. And on top of these huge subsidies, agribusiness has economies of scale and the market power to press suppliers for lower prices, which lets them operate profitably while family farmers are going broke. Not surprisingly, big farms are gobbling up small ones at a rapid pace, with considerable help from our taxpayer-supplied billions.

I don't begrudge anyone making money. But why should we keep silent while our government hews to a senseless and incredibly destructive policy that wastes billions of taxpayer dollars to support wrongheaded agricultural methods? Meanwhile, Earth-nurturing, sustainable practices are ignored. Many family farmers feel that their government has intentionally tossed them onto the trash heap, and they are correct.

What Can Go Right

All of my experiences have informed the way we deal with farmers at Stonyfield, and I am pleased to say that our approach has served both us and them well. In return for their dependable output and quality, and their promise to keep selling their milk to us, we pay our dairy farmers a floor price that we won't ever lower. This protects them from risk—that is, the unpredictability of everything from oil supplies to weather that affects commodity milk prices and leaves conventional dairies vulnerable to crazy swings in income. Sometimes, we pay two and a half times what conventional farmers receive; at other times, the premium may be only about 50 percent—which is still a lot, and makes them extremely loyal to us.

Over the years, as our business grew, so did our need for additional ingredients—sugar, cocoa, fruit, and so on—which depended on an ever larger number of farmers, some of them in distant lands. We hoped that if we treated all of them the same way we treated our dairy farmers, they would provide us with a steady supply of the best possible ingredients for our yogurt. And if we gave them the incentives to practice sustainable farming methods, we would, in fact, be investing in the equity of the Earth. Our experience convinced me that all companies, no matter what their industry, could profit by following our example.

Consider the record for organic milk prices. Between 1989 and 2006, the organic price rose almost steadily from $14.30 per hundredweight to $22.50 per hundredweight, a 57 percent increase over the past seventeen years, and 83 percent more than conventional farmers received in 2006. Organic demand has been growing faster than the supply, and consumers have not balked at paying more for healthier and—many of us believe—tastier products.

In fact, consumer demand in recent years has been growing by 20 percent or more annually, so much that there has been an actual shortage of organic milk. Some retailers have had to post notices in their dairy cases apologizing for not being able to provide enough. At Stonyfield, we had to briefly convert some organic products, like smoothies, to conventional.

You might think that much demand, plus the premium prices for organic, would induce a lot of farmers to switch to organic production. But the transition of cows takes a year, during which time a farmer has to turn his animals out to pasture or feed them with higher-priced organic feed (produced without chemical fertilizer or pesticides). He also has to do without antibiotics or growth hormone, which works fine in the long run but can cause problems during the changeover. And for that whole year, of course, his milk is fetching only conventional prices, in spite of his higher costs.

Converting to organic methods takes three years for fields. That's the legal minimum period of transition established by the USDA. While the land is transitioning and the farmer is learning how to follow organic practices, yields tend to drop, but will rise again as organic management improves soil health and fertility. That three-year transition imposes a limit on the growth of organic dairy farming: Any grower who wants to convert his land to organic and supply feed corn to an organic dairy, for instance, is likely to face decreased yields for a few years. That's a major disincentive, especially when corn farmers are planting every available acre to meet the demand of ethanol producers.

Despite these challenges, a great many dairy farmers have been thinking seriously about going organic, and a change in the rules produced a kind of organic rush in 2006. Before June 2006, farmers beginning the switch could feed their cows 80 percent organic feed during the first nine months, supplementing it with 20 percent conventional feed until the final three months of the conversion. Since the deadline, cows in transition must be fed 100 percent organic feed for the entire year. The cost difference is significant, so literally hundreds of dairy farmers decided to go organic in time to beat the deadline.

Obviously, no one can guarantee a constant rate of earnings growth or predict exact margins on sustainable or organic raw materials and products. But I am certain that organic methods hold out the best hope for the small farmer.

Look at some of Stonyfield's suppliers. The Gates family, for example, lives a life that many would envy on a 230-acre Vermont farm. Members of the Organic Valley Co-op, Karen and Jonathan, their three sons, and Jonathan's parents tend to 110 Jersey cows, the milk from which provides a predictable year-round income. We buy the milk for our yogurt from Organic Valley because it is a cooperative strictly comprised of family farmers. But diversity is the heart of organic farming, and the Gateses have taken to it with gusto, supplementing their income with a range of activities. Everyone lends a hand, including the youngsters, who accept their daily chores as a matter of course.

The family's seasonal pursuits include maple syrup production in the spring, poultry farming in the summer, a Christmas-tree business in the fall, and selling firewood in the winter. The winter job of managing the wood lot is not particularly demanding, so the Gateses are able to find time for a favorite family pleasure, cross-country skiing. The daily, multigenerational interaction and the lessons the boys learn from being responsible for specific chores are reminiscent of a time that most of us can barely imagine, let alone recall.

Another farmer I know was ready to give up after an eight-year struggle using conventional methods. Even though they had little more than a minimum-wage job to look forward to, he discouraged his kids from even considering farming. Then the Vermont Land Trust bought the development rights to his property. With that financial cushion, he has been able to convert to organic farming and is excited about the prospects. He is even looking to buy another farm, and is delighted that his four children are themselves interested in organic farming.

The price that Stonyfield pays its farmers has changed their lives and strengthened our company. But it goes beyond buying. We work together to improve our farmers' soil; Stonyfield has funded grants that promote better composting methods, and provides new fencing for rotational grazing and other benefits that make for mutual trust and loyalty. Freed of the suspicions that typically define supplier-customer relationships, our company and our farmers are able to collaborate on a scale that resembles, fittingly enough, one of nature's healthy ecosystems.

As a symbol of the love and respect we have for farmers and the faith we have in organic methods, my wife, Meg, and I personally joined with Stonyfield Farm and Organic Valley to create a $300,000 conversion loan fund that helps farmers through the transition year. It's touch and go until you come out the other side. We thought that this juncture was the perfect place for us to lend a hand.

Meg and I have long admired the New Hampshire Community Loan Fund and the work it does to promote affordable housing and economic opportunity in our state while staving off unwanted development. It's been around for more than twenty years and has invested $85 million in all manner of development projects. So we set up our organic-conversion lending pool as an arm of that organization. Meg, who shares my gratitude to the farmers and others who helped nurture the growth of Stonyfield, likes to think of our $300,000 contribution as "a way to keep the energy flowing round and round." She felt that helping to keep farmers afloat during a very difficult conversion year was only right, especially since these are the folks who work so hard to keep Stonyfield supplied with local milk. Finding a meaningful way to give back to our neighbors and the state of New Hampshire was very important to both of us.

Raising Cane in Brazil

We have much in common with all of our suppliers, whether they be dairymen or dirt farmers. We all think of ourselves as caretakers of a planet that our children and grandchildren must care for in their turn.

And this conviction knows no geographic or cultural boundaries; in fact, no supplier exemplifies it better than Leontino Balbo, the Brazilian sugarcane grower who has sold Stonyfield organic sugar for over a decade. "You have to give nature an opportunity to participate in the stewardship of the soil," Balbo says. "We treat our farms as a living organism, while most conventional farmers treat their farms as being sick."

Balbo's family has been in the sugar business ever since his grandfather, the son of Italian immigrants, went to work in a sugar mill at the age of nine. His sons followed him, and pooled their savings in 1947 to build their own mill and slowly become players in the giant industry. But it was in the mid-1980s that Leontino and his brothers and cousins grew up and joined the company, and made the hard decision to go organic. It was a tough transition; yields fell at first, and "People told me, 'You are going to ruin the family business,'" Leontino recently recalled. But in the end, his family's 49,400 acres of farmland turn in some of the most abundant harvests in all of the sugar-rich state of Sao Paolo, and he sells the organic sugar at a premium to customers including Smuckers, Starbucks, Stonyfield, and many other large organic brands around the world.

The younger generation's first revolutionary idea was that the monoculture of the cane fields was an unhealthy environment, and they determined to reintroduce biological diversity and sustainable methods to improve the quality of the sugar. They began in 1986 by reforesting patches of land among the sugar fields to create islands of biodiversity and rebalance the ecosystem. So far, they have planted more than 1 million trees—and as native vegetation grew from 5 percent of the plantation to about 14 percent, wild animals have returned and the food chain has been restored.

With Leontino as agricultural director of the company, the

partners learned to use organic management instead of chemicals. They also replaced pesticides with ingenious biological controls, cultivating a special fungus to eradicate leafhoppers and releasing millions of tiny wasps to fight the cane borer. But the most difficult part of the project was converting the dirty, dangerous business of hand-cutting cane to a clean, green, mechanized process that is taking over the industry.

Traditionally, the standing sugarcane is first burned, to strip its leaves, soften the stalks, and drive away insects and snakes. Then workers cut it with machetes. The burned cane oozes sap, which collects dirt as it contacts the ground, and the whole sticky, sooty, dirt-encrusted mass is hauled off to the mill. "We couldn't accept that," Balbo says. "We wanted the green sugarcane, not the burned one. We thought we had to improve the process." But it took five years, working with equipment makers, to develop a harvesting machine that would cut the cane neatly, top and bottom, shredding the remnants and strewing them around as compost to help fertilize the fields and keep them moist. Milling green cane also saves hundreds of thousands of gallons of water a day that would normally be used to wash the dirty burned cane.

By 1995, the harvest was all green. The first 1,600 tons of organic sugar were milled in 1997. Five years later, production zoomed to 23,000 tons. Today, the Native Green Cane Project can produce 80,000 tons of organic cane sugar a year. Approximately 70 percent is exported. The Balbo family is determined to expand the organic production to other mills in the group. And it's a financial bonanza: Organic sugar costs substantially more than conventional sugar to produce, but it commands three times the price at Brazil's supermarkets.

Balbo's sugar is all the sweeter for the care he puts into it—and many of his customers also understand that helping the planet is good for a company's own bottom line.

Newman's Own Goes Organic

The concept of fair trade, which began in the world's coffee fields and guarantees small family farmers a premium price and direct financing if needed, is increasingly popular. More than five hundred U.S. companies have latched onto the label, promoting fair-trade-certified coffee beans. So has my friend Nell Newman, the co-founder of Newman's Own Organics: The Second Generation. The daughter of actors Paul Newman and Joanne Woodward, she is deeply committed to organically grown foods, sustainable methods of agriculture, and the socioeconomic benefits that accrue to organic farmers. By selling more than sixty organic products, Nell stands up for the environment and sustainable farming methods. Royalties from Newman's Own Organics have gone, via the Newman's Own Foundation, to fund projects like an organic chicken operation in Oaxaca, Mexico, that helps women boost their household income and add protein to their family diets.

Nell inherited her respect for the environment and her social awareness from her parents. Joanne Woodward has long been known as a dedicated social and political crusader, and Paul Newman's corporate philanthropy is renowned: He has now donated more than $200 million in profits from his various food businesses to charitable causes. No child of Beverly Hills, Nell was raised in the Connecticut countryside. She recalls playing in the woods, fishing with her father and eating the catch, making applesauce with her mother using apples from the Newmans' own trees, tending chickens, and sampling all sorts of locally grown produce from the family garden and nearby farm stands.

After earning a degree in human ecology from the College of the Atlantic in Bar Harbor, Maine, Nell initially channeled her energies into jobs with the Environmental Defense Fund and the Ventana Wilderness Sanctuary in California. But after a stint fund-raising for the Santa Cruz Predatory Bird Research Group, she decided it was time to follow in her father's footsteps, both in business and in philanthropy.

Nell and her business partner, Peter Meehan, started their organic foods business as a division of her father's company, Newman's Own, in 1993. "Pop" or "Pa," as Nell sometimes calls the Oscar-winning actor, wasn't keen at first on the idea of adding an organic line to his food company. Like many people, she says, he thought organic food was bland and unappealing. So one Thanksgiving, Nell, who usually cooks for the family on holidays, made turkey, stuffing, mashed potatoes, and all the trimmings. Everything was organic, but she didn't mention it to her father until he was polishing off second helpings. "How did you like your organic Thanksgiving dinner?" she asked mischievously. The point was made, and Newman was soon writing the checks Nell and Peter needed to launch the business.

Newman's Own Organics, which has since become an independent company, was successful from the start, proving once again that there is money to be made in sustainable agriculture, both for the growers and the companies they supply. The company made enough money in just one year to enable Nell and Peter to pay back every cent of the start-up money borrowed from her father. Paul Newman expected repayment so he could funnel the money into the charities he supports.

The first product under the Newman's Own Organics label, an organic pretzel, became an almost instant hit. Nell followed up with an organic chocolate bar; she was drawn to the product, she says, when she learned of a new way to grow cacao that would not harm the rain forests. "We want to encourage this method by supporting the farmers who use it," she explains. Like me, Nell believes that anything one can do to help the world's impoverished farmers is worth doing.

Conventional coffee growers, like conventional dairy farmers, never know what they will be paid for their beans. The trading prices fluctuate wildly. And when coffee prices fall below production costs, the farmers are often forced to rely on unscrupulous lenders to keep them afloat until the next season. Many end up losing their land, their homes, and their possessions.

But with guaranteed, above-market pricing, coupled with the opportunity to get low-cost loans from a growers' cooperative when needed to tide people over till harvest, the fair-trade movement affords the world's poorest farmers a chance to live a better life. They can provide medical care for themselves and their families, educate their children, and, hopefully, lift themselves out of poverty. Perhaps the best news is that fair-trade practices are being extended to the growers of bananas, mangoes, cocoa, tea, and other foodstuffs, as well as to artisans making a wide range of goods for export.

Nell witnessed firsthand the benefits of fair trade in her visit not long ago to Guatemala. Flying in, she could see numerous abandoned coffee farms. It didn't take long to figure out that fair-trade pricing made the difference between those who were making a living and those who weren't.

Organic Valley, Where Healthy Foods Make Happy People

A revolution is taking shape in rural communities all across America. In twenty-six states, an organization of 1,100-plus farm families are doing much more than just making a living as they turn out a brimming market basket of foods. As members of the Organic Valley Family of Farms, a thriving, Wisconsin-based organic cooperative, these producers of ham, eggs, milk, and orange juice are making a life that many of them once thought no longer possible.

Young people like Travis Forgues are going back to the farm even after they've seen Paris (or, in Travis's case, St. Michael's College and a job in social services). And Organic Valley is cheering on the returning farmers and arming them with the economic opportunities they need to make a go of their ventures.

Organic Valley's mission is two-pronged: It aims to keep family farms alive, and to keep our planet healthy. Calling itself the "un-corporation," it works to achieve those ends by combining two business methods—the admired-but-endangered independent, single-family farm lifestyle and the democratically elected, farmer-run cooperative model that pools products to boost market clout and provide more financial stability. By employing collective-bargaining methods to ensure fair prices for farmers, and then channeling their production to local markets, Organic Valley is helping to change the face of both agriculture and food consumption in America. As a result, once-dying rural communities from Maine to Wisconsin to Washington State have reason to hope for an economic rebirth.

Founded in 1988 as a small organization called the Cooperative Regions of Organic Producer Pools, or CROPP, Organic Valley today supplies Stonyfield with milk for our yogurt and is the largest organic farmers' co-op in North America. All told, it currently enjoys $334 million worth of business annually and is growing rapidly, marketing more than 200 certified organically grown food items that include meat, milk, eggs, cheese, butter, juice, produce, and soy beverages. Its success is a testament both to the leadership of chief executive officer George Siemon, one of the seven founding farmers, and to the hard work and enthusiastic dedication of its 1,100 small and midsize family-farm members, particularly young missionaries like Travis Forgues.

Travis, of Alburg Springs, Vermont, perched near the tip of Lake Champlain on the Canadian border, originally took the advice of his beleaguered parents and in 1991 left dairy farming behind for college and a career working with at-risk youths. But whenever he thought about his future and the possibility of a family, Travis couldn't picture raising kids anywhere other than in the country. So, in 1995, he and his wife, Amy, returned to Alburg Springs and began farming with Travis's parents.

Intrigued by organic farming methods he'd heard about while in college, Travis had little trouble convincing his father to make the switch to sustainable agriculture. Henry Forgues, no stranger to the financial hardships of conventional farming, had already adopted pastured dairying methods in the late 1980s as a way to save money on feed. And because he had also shunned chemical pesticides and herbicides and the drugs used to make cows give more milk, the father-son venture was well along in its switch to organic farming when an Organic Valley representative came calling in 1997. Not long after hearing that we at Stonyfield, along with other New England–based dairy-product manufacturers, were buying milk from Organic Valley—and paying a premium price for it—the Forgues signed up as farmer-owners in CROPP.

Soon, Travis was out preaching the financial benefits of CROPP membership to his neighbors, while also extolling the environmental virtues of pasture-based feeding and farming. Today, 121 Vermont farmers and their families, who might otherwise have lost their land, are successfully managing 6,050 cows on 22,900 acres under the Organic Valley Family of Farms umbrella. The milk they produce brings in nearly twice the conventional price. As word of their success has spread, the waiting list in Vermont has come to resemble the line to purchase a Powerball lottery ticket—except that sustainable converts are virtually guaranteed to win.

The Organic Valley story is much the same all across the country. Young people are leaving cities behind to return to their rural roots, and even some inexperienced newcomers are taking a chance on a way of life thought done for decades ago—all because of a burgeoning interest in organic eggs, meat, produce, and especially milk.

Now farmers are being offered free grain, veterinary care, and other incentives to help them switch from conventional methods to organic dairy farming. Stonyfield and Organic Valley set aside $2 million in the summer of 2006 to help bring more farmers into the fold. Organic Valley recently opened a new $17.5 million, ecologically friendly distribution warehouse in Cashton, Wisconsin, which attests to the co-op's growth, its commitment to making farm communities economically viable, and its deep-seated concern for the environment.

George Siemon refers to himself as Organic Valley's C-E-I-E-I-O. George and his family have been running their own organic operation since 1977. Their crops are grown free of chemicals that might harm consumers and threaten the health of the planet, while animals are treated ethically and humanely, a prerequisite for meats sold under the co-op's Organic Prairie brand.

For many farmers, treating animals humanely is simply the right thing to do, and if it also entices animal-loving consumers to purchase certified products that command higher prices, so much the better. But regardless of motive, humane treatment is definitely good business. As Travis Forgues recently explained, "What we've found is that if you treat your animals with a little respect, feed them ten pounds of grain and hay, and ask them to do what they can do, they stay healthy." In other words, veterinary bills will be far lower, production higher, and profits larger. Sounds like a simple decision to me: Where's the downside?

Between caring for his fields and livestock and spreading the gospel of sustainable agriculture, George Siemon has somehow found the time to lead the drive to develop and enforce honest and workable standards for organic certification. A past member of the U.S. Department of Agriculture's small farm advisory committee, he now helps the USDA decide which ingredients and farming practices can rightly be labeled organic.

George expresses concern over proliferating efforts to market meat under such labels as "free farmed" and "cage free," which haven't been vetted by the USDA but seem to imply something better than organic. He notes that current organic standards already protect animals by demanding outdoor access for livestock and banning cages for egg-laying hens. He's also bothered by another dispute over organic milk that pits small family dairy farmers against big corporate farms, some milking more than a thousand cows, that are rushing into the organic tent. Some purists argue that no big corporation has the right to call itself organic. But in George's opinion, size—either big or small—is no indicator of virtue. Big operators and small alike must follow the USDA guidelines. He thinks people are mixing up standards with cultural issues, and sees the size issue as nothing more than a market differentiator. Organic Valley doesn't want "to disparage other organic producers" or conventional ones either, he says. The co-op just wants to hammer home the positive aspects of its own brand.

When a once-moribund market segment explodes into a $17.7 billion-a-year (and expanding fast) opportunity, it's a safe bet that much of the infighting is the result of growing pains. But with its nineteen-year track record as a major champion of small family farmers and environmentally sound organic agricultural methods, it's an even safer bet that Organic Valley is on the right side of the argument.

I share George's point of view. If I go on and on about the soil-saving, health-giving, life-enhancing practices of family farmers, it's because I don't believe we can continue to exist on this Earth without them. I am emotionally as well as intellectually committed to saving family farms. But business runs on hard numbers, not emotion, and I'm also sure that Stonyfield hasn't lost any of its virtue as it has become bigger. If anything, the larger we grow, the more good we can do. In the next chapter, I share my vision of what I hope our country and our planet can become if business wakes up and seizes the profitable opportunity to operate sustainably.

8

Future Perfect

June 1, 2028

Nearly three decades into the twenty-first century, it's hard to believe how far we have come.

Almost twenty years ago, I stopped climbing Mount Washington, one of my favorite places on Earth. It was too painful. As an ecologist and skier, I once loved the highest (6,288 feet) peak in New Hampshire as a sort of anteroom to space. I studied its tree lines, home to fascinating species. I battled fierce winds. I savored air so clean and clear that on a sunny day you saw the Atlantic sparkling sixty miles away.

By 2008, this granite monument to pure nature was surrounded by pollution. Most days of the year the Atlantic was invisible, a mere rumor of past delights. I didn't want to know the fate of my tree-line creatures, or brave the diesel-belching buses that now sped overweight tourists up paved roads where we had once skied in powder snow. The real world was gone, erased by humans trashing their own home.

That was then: What a difference twenty years makes in the zigzag story of human enlightenment. Who knew that our capacity for self-renewal, so often given up for dead, would rise again to save us from our worst instincts?

Let's not dwell on that dismal era when despair surged like lava and the devil himself appeared in charge. Let's savor our amazing progress. Two decades later, the world has not ended with a gaseous whimper. It has instead responded to global warming with astonishingly sane antidotes that each month improve our odds for survival. It now appears possible, if not yet definite, that our children will in fact escape the abyss toward which our own generation once blindly drove humanity, dragging our fellow species behind us in clouds of toxic dust.

About 30 percent of China's industrial areas now have healthy air, compared with 12 percent two years ago. Global temperature dropped half a degree last year. The climate is improving. Arctic ice packs, glaciers, and ocean levels are stabilizing. Hurricane seasons are no longer completely dreaded again.

Future historians will see all this more clearly than we do, but one can speculate that our peril and our rescue both arose from the same cause, humanity's headlong conquest of nature and our assumed superiority over all other forms of life. Spurred by vast strides in myriad technologies, from agriculture to medicine, from air-conditioning to information, the human population exploded, creating a global economy split into the very rich and the very poor. As the twenty-first century began, the world felt literally smaller, overcrowded, dangerous—prone to contagious terrorism, waves of refugees, religious hatred, drug-immune diseases.

When the Internet enabled an Earth-shrinking global economy, the fallout often had a Jekyll-and-Hyde quality. It was good news for Americans that fast jetliners allowed more than 130 countries to ship perishable food to the United States. It was grim news that Washington's budget-minders slashed the United States Food and Drug Administration's inspection staff. Charged with monitoring 80 percent of U.S. food, the agency could screen only about 1 percent of imports arriving at hundreds of American entries. As a result, U.S. restaurants and supermarkets unwittingly sold products tainted with toxic pesticides or preservatives. At one point, thousands of American cats and dogs were sickened by Chinese pet food reportedly thickened with melamine, a resin used in plastics. And it turned out the same food was fed to chickens, who were subsequently slaughtered and sold in supermarkets.

Such episodes came at a time when soaring global trade threatened to spread food-borne diseases previously limited to local areas, back when the world was bigger. Humans were now increasingly vulnerable to life-threatening ailments, such as avian flu, E. coli, and mad cow disease.

The most troubling effect of a smaller world was, of course, global warming, caused by too many humans spewing CO_2 into the atmosphere, overheating the Earth, thawing its polar icecaps, and flooding whole coastlines. Fortunately, the world's new smallness also helped ameliorate the crisis. Mass news media alarms plus Al Gore's 2006 film, *An Inconvenient Truth,* quickly saturated the planet. Record-breaking heat and hurricanes did the rest. Hardly anyone doubted that worldwide action was imperative.

The doubters, however, included certain large energy companies and their political allies, then occupying the White House. Until they finally saw the light—too late to retain the presidency—their opposition to real CO_2 controls impeded progress and weakened reformers, leaving ordinary citizens confused and frustrated. What to do?

It is true that on occasion, vast numbers of concerned citizens produce unexpected social changes. Self-interest can indeed trump the most stubborn bad habits. Overnight, New Yorkers began cleaning up after their dogs. Fear of lung cancer transformed a nation of smokers. But global warming was the bad habit of an entire global culture, too big for individuals to change effectively. Only business could do it. The good news is that it has.

I couldn't imagine it back in 2008, but companies now hold themselves accountable not only for the financial costs of doing business, but for all the carbon costs of all their operations. They share it with their customers: Every product has a label itemizing its manufacturer's carbon impact. Companies strive to reduce the impact, and customers overwhelmingly favor products with labels showing minimal or no impact.

In turn, business-inspired offsets allow any concerned individual to help rebuild America's energy infrastructure. In the upper Midwest, for example, powerful winds sweeping the plains can potentially supply one-third of all U.S. energy needs. Accordingly, six Native American tribes in the region built a vast wind enterprise called Native Electric Wind (NEW). The business is partly financed by average Americans buying RECs (renewable energy credits). These are tax-deductible additions to their electric bills, which are passed on to NativeEnergy. Under federal law, wind generators can use RECs to force conventional utilities to buy their power in the REC amounts. Result: Utilities duly reduce fossil fuels; more windmills get built; individual donors get a chance to make a difference.

Best and most effective of all, businesses simultaneously discovered that the market for low-carbon products and processes was potentially far bigger than the suddenly dwindling customer base for boondoggles like beachfront houses, gas-drunk SUVs, oil furnaces, and smoke-belching factories. The most astounding change, of course, resulted from the public's almost pandemic revolt against fossil fuels as a clear and present danger to national security. This crippled the once-arrogant oil majors. Demand fell, creating an oil surplus and a price plunge from $125 a barrel to $15. I can't even begin to analyze the political and diplomatic fallout from the parallel decline of U.S. dependence on Middle Eastern oil.

Enter hot competition, the economic genie enabling free markets to have their restorative way. We now saw frantic oil companies battling public utilities for market share in developing the petrocracy's former no-no's, such as wind farms and hydrogen or solar energy. In response, utilities like Con Edison and Florida Power & Light polished their "clean energy" images by recovering methane gas from sewage, developing liquefied coal, and perfecting solar panels, which real-estate developers quickly adopted as customer-grabbers, causing an upheaval in real estate values.

In a similar vein, Ford survived its near-death years by

launching its H2O, a sharp new family sedan that runs on hydrogen and emits nothing more toxic than water. Close behind, General Motors finally stole a march on Toyota by unveiling a sexy American sports car made of lightweight composites, with a radical new engine able to speed 150 miles on one gallon of gas, and a bumper-to-bumper warranty on all parts for twenty years. Carbon impact: near-zero.

The ramifications of carbon detoxification keep going on and on. Take the insurance industry. With less risk of coastal flooding and hurricanes, the industry has recouped massive losses, agreed to insure builders for the still-unfinished construction of New Orleans (after Katrina II), and become a hot sector for investors. And speaking of investors, we now have a whole new class of clean-energy billionaires, notably those who spotted early opportunities in alternate energy methods that really worked, such as geothermal and hydroelectric power.

Meantime, the rediscovery of organic farming has done wonders to revive the American family farm, long thought obliterated by giant agribusinesses. To that unexpected comeback we can add a surprising upsurge in business honesty. Today's customers and investors demand total transparency from the companies they patronize, and they seem to be getting it. Probably inspired by America's growing insistence on pure food, and enabled by information technology, new bar codes and labels trace every product's origin and environmental impact as mercilessly as a police blotter. Leery of this week's special on chickens? Consult your BlackBerry.10 for the complete biography of a specific bird going all the way back to its birth weight, where it was raised, and what it was fed. Not sure about a seductive-sounding dish on a Chinese menu? Not to worry: The waiter's little readout machine churns out all ingredients, their origins in Guangzhou, the recipe, and when the chef finished your order. In other words, you can be your own FDA inspector and feel quite confident that food-borne illness, though always possible, is now highly unlikely. American food has never been fresher or safer.

To top it all, food joins nearly all other products in having never been packaged more intelligently and with less environmental impact. No more oil-based plastic bags littering the landscape, poisoning the air when burned. No more impenetrable blister packaging that only a safecracker can open. In many cases, modern packaging is not only minimal, but biodegradable.

What a miracle business has wrought! Market incentives have forced chemical companies like Monsanto to diversify; inspired McDonald's to recycle its global rivers of French fry grease into new car fuels through its subsidiary, McFuels; discredited artificial sweeteners while reviving Latin America's sugar growers; and slashed health insurance costs for employers as Americans reject obesity, eat better, and live longer. Not surprisingly, Wall Street has amply rewarded low-carbon companies, and the country's horrendous Medicare costs have suddenly begun to look controllable.

What a difference two decades of business innovation and competition make in a truly noble challenge—reordering America's priorities and combating planetary suicide in the process.

Tomorrow morning, despite an aging left knee, I am joining

my grandchildren for a celebratory hike on Mount Washington along the old ski trail up to Tuckerman Ravine. The forecast is for a warm, glorious June morning with maximum visibility. I plan to dampen any lingering doubts and see what I came for—a sweeping, carbon-free glance all sixty miles southeast to the shining Atlantic Ocean.

Afterword

Now that you've made your way through this book, you may be wondering: What's next?

That question reminds me of the joke about whether it's worse to be ignorant or apathetic, to which the answer is, of course: "I don't know and I don't care."

But I believe that you do care, which is why you've stuck with me to the end. And because I also believe in the singular power of you, I humbly suggest that you can make a difference right now—and without adding anything to your already overburdened plate of daily responsibilities. All you need to do, if you haven't already, is to shift your purchases to products and services offered by companies that are working to reduce their climate footprints. To get started, fire up your computer and go to ClimateCounts.org. And if possible, let retailers know your preferences for sustainable products. An e-mail or text message to the companies themselves, whether to praise or threaten, can have an immense impact. But just letting them know you've got the planet in mind when you shop can literally change the world.

Do you think I'm crazy? If you've gotten this far, you know I am—crazy for this planet we live on. Winston Churchill said that success is the ability to move from failure to failure with no loss of enthusiasm. I plead guilty. But I prefer my much missed friend Anita Roddick's line that "Anyone who thinks he is too small to make a difference has never been in bed with a mosquito."

No matter which quotation you identify with, I have one simple question for you: What have you got to lose? We all turn into compost sooner or later, so we might as well feel good about how we live our lives while we are here.

Being cynical is pointless and a terrible way to live. Conversely, true happiness comes, I believe, from knowing that you've made a difference in the world. And if the experience I had a few months ago is any indication, the rewards are almost indescribable.

Recently, I was standing in a Florida supermarket reading the label on a Yoplait yogurt cup because I was curious about a new ingredient the company was trying. An older customer walked over to me, touched me on the elbow, and said, "Young man, someone your age really should be eating the Stonyfield." Her comment was akin to a religious moment for me. However, I regained my composure quickly enough to ask why she thought I should be eating the Stonyfield product. Her remarkably well-informed answer can be summarized this way: Since I apparently have a few decades left in me, I can make them more enjoyable and productive by eating organic foods. Plus, I will get the extra bonus of knowing that I am supporting a company that cares. This lovely woman certainly sold me.

I never take even a single moment of life on this Earth for granted, particularly since I lost my twin brothers five years ago. They were near their fortieth birthday when they died from congenital heart defects. Since then, I have also kept in mind an oft-spoken line of an old colleague, Itzak Adizes, who liked to say that we can't take life too seriously because it is just a temporary condition.

The truth is that we've all got a limited time in which to do something useful on this Earth. The present is but a nexus between past and future. And at this moment, we are blessed to be in an age that offers access to reams of data showing that humankind's past ignorance of nature's bountiful examples of sustainability has led to abysmal failure. Now, as we reject those misguided approaches in favor of trying to live in harmony with nature and providing a healthier world for our children, it is equally clear that the twenty-first century poses incredible opportunities for all of us to channel lessons learned into truly restorative and sustainable commerce.

Someone once said, "I don't know what the future holds, but I do know who holds it." You can find the answer by looking in the nearest mirror. Begin your journey toward a brighter future by making your next commercial activity a consciously sustainable one. Your grandchildren will thank you for stirring it up.

Gary Hirshberg
June 2007
Londonderry, New Hampshire

Index

Stonyfield Farm
ORGANIC
fat free
FRENCH VANILLA
smooth & creamy
Stonyfield Farm
ORGANIC
lowfat
BLUEBERRY
fruit on the bottom

ORGANIC
Stonyfield Farm
ORGANIC
Smoothie
A REFRESHING
DRINKABLE
LOWFAT YOGURT
STRAWBERRY

Save $2.00 on FOUR (4) 6 oz. Cups of
Stonyfield Farm Organic Yogurt

Retailer: For each coupon you accept as an authorized agent we will pay you $2.00 plus 8 cents handling. Invoices proving purchase of sufficient stock to cover all coupons redeemed must be shown upon request. Cash value 1/20 cent. Redeem by mail to: Stonyfield Farm, Inc. CMS Dept. #52159, One Fawcett Drive, Del Rio, TX 78840.

Save $2.00 on FOUR (4) 10 oz.
Stonyfield Farm Organic Smoothies

Retailer: For each coupon you accept as an authorized agent we will pay you $2.00 plus 8 cents handling. Invoices proving purchase of sufficient stock to cover all coupons redeemed must be shown upon request. Cash value 1/20 cent. Redeem by mail to: Stonyfield Farm, Inc. CMS Dept. #52159, One Fawcett Drive, Del Rio, TX 78840.

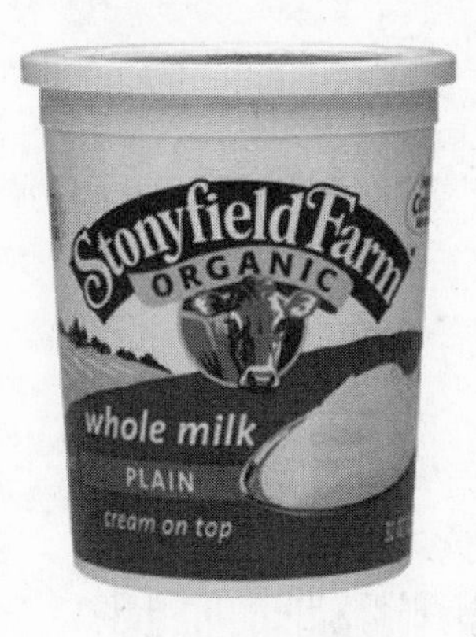

Stonyfield Farm
ORGANIC
whole milk
PLAIN
cream on top

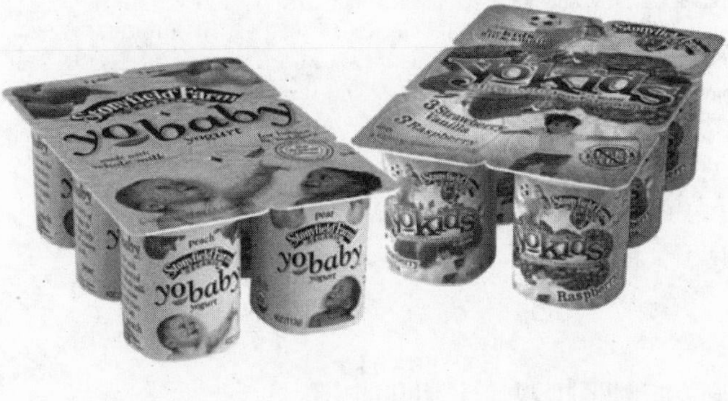
Stonyfield Farm
yobaby
peach
pear
YoKids
3 Strawberry Vanilla
3 Raspberry
Raspberry

Save $1.00 on ONE (1) 32 oz. Cup of Stonyfield Farm Organic Yogurt

Retailer: For each coupon you accept as an authorized agent we will pay you $1.00 plus 8 cents handling. Invoices proving purchase of sufficient stock to cover all coupons redeemed must be shown upon request. Cash value 1/20 cent. Redeem by mail to: Stonyfield Farm, Inc. CMS Dept. #52159, One Fawcett Drive, Del Rio, TX 78840.

Save $1.00 on ONE (1) Stonyfield Farm YoBaby or YoKids Organic Yogurt Multipack

Retailer: For each coupon you accept as an authorized agent we will pay you $1.00 plus 8 cents handling. Invoices proving purchase of sufficient stock to cover all coupons redeemed must be shown upon request. Cash value 1/20 cent. Redeem by mail to: Stonyfield Farm, Inc. CMS Dept. #52159, One Fawcett Drive, Del Rio, TX 78840.

Stonyfield Farm
ORGANIC
Organic
Lowfat Milk
1% Milkfat
Ultra-Pasteurized • Vitamins A&D

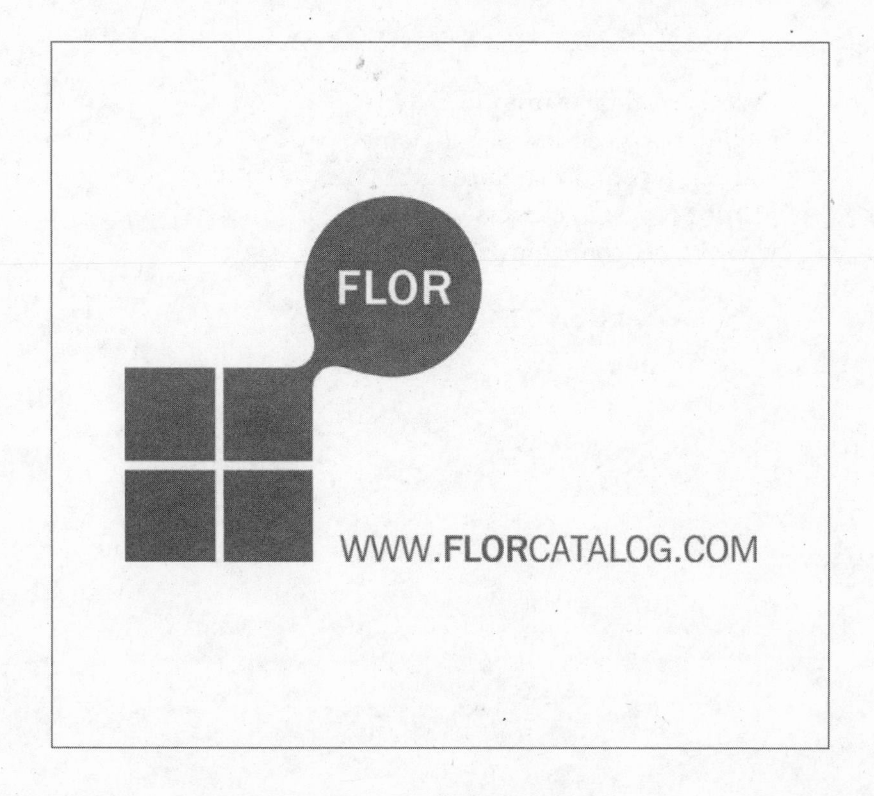
FLOR
WWW.FLORCATALOG.COM

seventh
GENERATION
™

ORGANIC
VALLEY
Family of Farms

$1.00 Off Any Seventh Generation Product

Retailer: For each coupon you accept as an authorized agent we will pay you a maximum of $1.00 plus 8 cents handling. Invoices proving purchase of sufficient stock to cover all coupons redeemed must be shown upon request. Cash value 1/20 cent. Redeem by mail to: Seventh Generation, Inc. CMS Dept. #32913. One Fawcett Drive, Del Rio, TX 78840. Limit one per customer. Void where prohibited. No doubling. Customer must pay any sales tax. Expires December 31, 2012.

$1.00 Off Any Organic Valley Product
"Local, Organic, & Farmer-Owned as Good as It Gets"

Expiration Date 1/31/2013. Consumer: Coupon good only in USA on purchase of brand/size indicated. Void if copied, transferred, prohibited or regulated. Retailer: Limit one coupon per purchase. Consumer to pay sales tax. We will reimburse you for face value of this coupon plus 8 cents handling if redeemed in compliance with our redemption policy. Copy sent upon request. Cash value 1/100 cents. Mail coupon to: CMS, Dept. 93966, 1 Fawcett Dr, Del Rio TX 78840. DO NOT DOUBLE.

Timberland